92

AMAZING APPS
FOR TEACHERS

And **EXACTLY** How to Use Them!

Dr. Kipp Rogers & Jamie Hall

With a Foreword from
Dr. Jordan Reeves Walker

92 AMAZING APPS FOR TEACHERS
and EXACTLY How to Use Them
Dr. Kipp Rogers and Jamie Hall

Copyright© 2012
ISBN 978-0-9838516-3-9

JULIANJOHN

JulianJohn Publishing

92 Amazing Apps for Teachers is an independent publication and has not been authorized, sponsored, or otherwise approved by Apple Inc. Apple®, iPad®, iPhone®, iPod®, iBooks®, and iBookstore® are registered trademarks of Apple Inc.

The names of individual apps featured in this publication are trademarks and the property of the companies or individuals who developed them. Neither the authors nor the publisher are affiliated with the companies referenced herein, and they will not assume any liability for their use, effectiveness, availability, or performance.

Cover Design by Sean O'Connor
www.OhSeeDesign.com

Printed in the United States of America

Foreword from
Dr. Jordan Reeves Walker...

Greetings!

It gives me great pleasure to introduce you to two of the most amazing educators you will meet anywhere: Dr. Kipp Rogers and Jamie D. Hall.

Together, they have compiled a list of amazing apps that you can use tomorrow in your classroom to increase motivation and learning.

As I have watched the introduction of the iPad® in classrooms across the country in the past few years, a few trends have become quite obvious:

Teachers need help selecting good apps. This book is an essential tool in that process.

Apps alone do not increase learning. Apps coupled with good teaching can increase both motivation and learning.

Different apps fit into different situations. Some classrooms have just one iPad, while others have a few or even one iPad for every student. You will find many of the apps in this book fit into each of those situations, while others are unique to one setting.

This book is not organized like you might expect. Rather than create sections of the book divided into different types of apps, we have intentionally presented the apps in a more random format. The reason for this is simple: Many times you don't know what you are looking for until you find it!

Let's be honest: One year before iPads were released to the public, NONE of us were sitting around wishing we had a tablet with a touch screen and only one button! But once we discovered the iPad... many of us cannot picture life without it.

We intentionally do not want you to look in this book for just one type of app. Our organizational structure (or lack thereof!) will allow you to discover apps that you will love ... even if you did not know you needed them!

I hope you enjoy this process of discovery as much as I do!

I offer my heartfelt thanks for Dr. Kipp Rogers and Jamie D. Hall for leading us on this journey!

Dr. Jordan Reeves Walker
www.DisciplineGuru.com

Introduction from
Jamie D. Hall...

Hello, Fellow Educators...

Welcome to *92 Amazing Apps for Teachers...and EXACTLY How to Use Them!*

With over 500,000 apps on the app store, you may have discovered, like me, that finding useful apps can be time consuming and frustrating. As teachers, we all know just how important our time is!! I've spent hours searching, downloading, reviewing and kid testing apps, saving you all that time!

I've helped hundreds of teachers in my district with EXACTLY how to use these apps in their classroom to increase student learning and creativity. I've improved the way teachers teach and the way they motivate students. This book will do the same for you! Whether you have one, several, or a class set of iPads, this book will help you get started on the right foot. I am so excited to share the apps in this book and how you can use them in your teaching.

Remember, iPads can't improve learning without your good teaching! Thanks!

Jamie D. Hall

Introduction from
Dr. Kipp Rogers...

Welcome to the wonderful world of apps!

For the past few years, I have watched hundreds of teachers use thousands of apps in their classrooms. This book will share the very BEST of those apps with YOU!

Thank you for taking the time to choose the very best for your students and for your willingness to embrace new technologies to increase student motivation and learning in your classroom!

Enjoy these amazing apps!

Dr. Kipp Rogers

Table of Contents

Bad Review

ABC News... Headlines World & US

1

3D Cell Stimulation and Stain Tool

They're small and hard to see, making them usually even more difficult to grasp and understand. Many students may moan and groan with the mention of them, but no longer! With the 3D Cell Stimulation and Stain Tool app, studying and learning the basic structures and functions of any cell is no longer complicated. In fact, it may even become a simple, fun, and interactive process. In any middle through high school science, biology, or biochemistry classroom, the convenience of this app can easily be put to use to increase the understanding of basic cell structure in a total hands-on way.

Through the app, you can view an actual digital cell in full 3D form. On top of this, you or a student may change the view of the entire cell to your preference. This includes, not only the rotation of the cell a full 360 degrees, but also the capability to zoom in and out. The easy movement in, around, and through the cell on the screen makes the computerized image a useful learning or studying tool for any science class.

Not only does 3D Cell Stimulation and Stain Tool provide an easily understood image, but it includes great descriptions for all of the structures within the cell. From a list within the app, you can select any of the structures that make up the cell. In these paragraphs, not only is the function of the structure explained, but it also features how it relates to all of the other structures of the cell. Along with the paragraph description, each page includes a video of the component. The video goes even more in depth with the explanation of the structure.

To take things further, the app also allows the creation of your very own cell stain. By using Molecular Probes products and personalization of the color of each structure of the cell, you are able to make a truly unique cell stain of your own. This feature also once more reinforces the various parts of the cell by making them stand out on their own, all individually. With the diverse options available, you can make over 250 different versions of your cell stain. This means enough for a new cell stain per student, allowing everyone to make one of their own. Once the cell is created, you may also send the cell to a friend, student, or fellow teacher to share or for further use.

Whether you're just starting a basic introduction of cells in a middle school classroom or diving deeply into the study of cells in high school, 3D Cell Stimulation and Stain Tool is a must for any science classroom. No matter whether a student uses this free app to pass the time or for true studying and learning, it can be a full intellectual experience. No longer will the topic of cell structures be met with moans and groans, but, instead, you will have a class full of kids who both grasp and understand their functions and relations to the other components of the cell—not to mention the hours of fun that can go into the creation of your very own cell stain.

Company: Invirtogen Corporation
Size: 32.5 MB
Rating: 3 stars
Grade Level: Middle School-High School

2

ABC News

New things happen every year, every month, every week, every day, every hour, and every second. Just because you and your students spend the entire day inside a school, it doesn't mean that the rest of the world presses the pause button. With modern technology at today's level, these new things are easily and quickly spread throughout the world like a wildfire. While the world keeps moving and you and your class are still isolated in your classroom, the use of the ABC News app allots you easy access to the outside world from your classroom, whether for discussion, current events, or both.

Upon opening the app, you are immediately met with a globe. Though shaped similar to the visual image that correlates with the word globe, your expected layout of our seven continents is no longer the surface image. Instead, the exterior of this sphere is covered with the newest and most recent news articles of the moment, with each article featuring a title and picture. With a stroke of your fingertips, you can easily spin the globe a full 360 degrees, showing yet even more of the day's top and most recent articles. One more simple tap to the image of the article, and the full story is brought to your device's screen.

By a minor settings change, you can also control exactly what types of articles appear on your main screen globe. Instead of the variety of articles shown by default, you can narrow down what appears to your favorite subjects, or the ones most useful to your classroom. Whether it is world news, politics, entertainment, science, or technology, you have full rein over the stories that will appear on your globe. You can also shake your device to shuffle the articles that are shown to be replaced with new ones of your topic selection.

13

Along with the written articles, the ABC News app also provides access to a variety of videos. These videos can be either their own stand-alone program or an attachment clip to another article. Either way, the footage can easily help elaborate the topic at hand. Furthermore, at various times, you can also watch breaking news and live events when they are available. A button will appear on the screen for you to press when streaming is available. While the constant access to all of these articles and videos requires Internet capabilities, you may also favorite any story by adding it to "My Favorites." With the article saved, you can easily take it with you for sharing outside of Internet access and on-the-go.

Whether your classroom consists of wound-up elementary aged kids or more mature high schoolers, students of all ages will be able to appreciate the ABC News app. If you're requiring discussion of the current events for any class, this free app can be easily integrated into any conversation. Students can also conveniently use it to look up the most recent stories for a homework assignment or project. The videos and live streaming options also provide another teaching tool or way to stay connected to the outer world during the work and school day.

Company: ABC Digital
Size: 8.4 MB
Rating: 3.5 Stars
Grade Level: All

3 *Good*

Animation Desk for iPad®

Kids and students of all ages have always been entertained for hours by drawing, whether they're good at it or not. Drawing just took its next step forward with the Animation Desk for iPad® app. Now ridding of the cost and mess left behind of markers and crayons, this app makes drawing and even animation a whole new experience for all ages and classrooms.

Animation Desk for iPad® creates an all the more hands-on feeling for drawing, while keeping the new modern technology aspect. The overall goal of the app is to allow you or your students to create an animation video, which can easily be used for fun or a project. The app features over 100 colors and adjustable brush sizes and opacity for both the colors and eraser. You can choose from pencils, crayons, three types of brushes, and an eraser. With these endless options, the possibility of making your very own animations becomes a reality. On top of using the brushes to create the lines of your drawings, you can also use the paint bucket tool to fill in large sections in a breeze. Best of all, the app has a palm rejection feature. This allows you to rest your palm of your hand on the screen, without activating other features or drawing unwanted lines.

Along with the expected features of a drawing or animation app, Animation Desk for iPad® takes things to the next level. For starters, you can either create a background of your own or choose from one of the predesigned backgrounds available. It is also an option to select a picture from your saved photo library to apply as the background. To make the drawing process even simpler, you may use the stamp tool within the app. This allows you to add basic shapes to your animation, insert more pictures from your library, or copy and paste already drawn sections of your image. While drawing, the app also features the ability to save a foreground and a middle ground. This lets you work and edit one level of the picture without affecting the other.

Once you have your basic animation images drawn, you can organize them into an animated video. You can add each frame to make a seamless show! Animation Desk for iPad® allows for easy editing, copying, moving, and deleting of all the frames in your animation story board. Besides the layout of these multiple frames, to make your animation even more your own, you can add background music throughout it. You may also include various sound effects throughout the show. When the animation show is finished, you can easily save it on the app to come back to later, while working on the other animations you have in progress. Through the app, you can easily save any of your animations in a PDF format or email them to other classrooms and students for viewing.

Any classroom, whether an actual computer applications class or any basic fundamental class who wants to tell a story about their lesson via animation, can easily incorporate Animation Desk for iPad® into their lesson plans. Unlimited amounts of projects and lessons could come out of this modernized traditional concept in a realistic manner. For only $4.99, this app could quickly become a new classroom favorite.

Company: Kdan Mobile Software LTP
Size: 39.6 MB
Rating: 4.5 Stars
Grade Level: All

4

Animoto Video Slideshow

You've got groups upon groups of students preparing to present their speeches. They all have the same types of PowerPoints—either boring white with black text or a rainbow of bright backgrounds that require squinting to read. None of them are original and all of them drag on, or maybe it's the other way around. Instead, it's you who has the repetitive slideshows that are all incapable of keeping your students' attention. With the Animoto Video Slideshow app, that will no longer be the problem, and original slideshows will quickly become the norm.

With the use of Animoto Video Slideshow, there is an easy solution to creating quick, professional presentations that both teacher and student can use. By first selecting pictures from your photo library, your presentation can be easily created and manipulated into any of your own desires. Whether you're studying architecture, sciences, art, or history, you can easily create a slideshow that is different than any your students have ever seen before. Along with adding photos into your show, you can also easily put in videos that correspond with the topic at hand.

To make your selection of pictures even more separate from a normal slideshow presentation, the app features multiple layouts of how the pictures and videos appear. These styles include more than your usual transitions, and more layouts are added with each update. Animoto Video Slideshow also features the option to add music to your presentation in a breeze. The endless amount of music options available in the app will provide almost any type of tune to suit nearly any topic or subject.

Additionally, you may also add words to the presentation. Since the video slideshows focus on the pictures, the option to add captions will make it even more original. The simplicity of the app will allow these original slides to be finished in little to no time. Previewing the slideshow while it's still in progress allows you to see where you are and how much you still have left to complete. When finished with the slideshow, you can save it through the app. It can then be viewed from the app itself or on their website. When viewing it from their website, you can also easily project it in the classroom for all the class to see. If you later realize that there is something that needs to be changed or added and you have already published and finalized it, you can easily go back, make changes, and resave it.

The next time class presentations come around, Animoto Video Slideshow is your go-to app. Instead of having students reading paragraphs contained in their slideshow screens, they now will have a photo-centered presentation. This allows them to speak more from their own knowledge, instead of the Internet. These pictures-gone-video presentations with full-out music and text can be the next step forward for all student projects and teacher lectures. All grade levels can use this free app to make classroom learning more fun and interesting.

Company: Animoto, Inc.
Size: 13.8 MB
Rating: 4.5 Stars
Grade Level: All

5
AppShopper

New apps are always added, but occasionally hard to find. Sometimes there are app sales, but it's difficult to tell exactly what kinds are available and hard to keep track of them all. Maybe it's overwhelming to look at your wish list of apps, or perhaps you want a notification the second your favorite classroom app has an update available. Whatever your story may be, it's no doubt the number of apps available is an overwhelming concept. No matter what types of apps you're seeking for your classroom, AppShopper makes the entire process a much simpler one.

Sometimes, with the numbers of apps available through the app store, it can be difficult to determine which ones are truly worth your time, especially when there are hundreds of apps all claiming to accomplish the same thing. Through AppShopper, you can easily view the top 200 apps. However, unlike the app store, where top apps are determined by most purchased, these top 200 are the most popular as decided by other AppShopper users. Finding the right apps for your classroom can become even simpler.

By favoriting apps or adding them to your wish list, you can also track them. By scrolling through a list you create in the app, you can easily watch what's happening with the apps you wish to have. Whether it is a permanent price drop or just a week-long sale, you can easily changes to any app you would find use for in your classroom. AppShopper also shows you a list of the newest apps available for download.

If you or your students have a favorite app, AppShopper also syncs with your Wish List and My Apps off of iTunes. Through the My Apps tab at the bottom, you can view all the apps you've already bought or downloaded onto your device. The list will look at the apps you have downloaded and tell you when there is an update available for any of them. Whether it's from your Favorite List or My Apps, you can sign up to get notifications via email or push notification. Push notifications will alert your actual device with any update. These updates could include price drops, a new version of any of your apps, or new apps that may interest you that have recently been added.

Within AppShopper, you can search through all the apps, like in the actual App Store. However, the app provides even more options. Besides viewing the Top 200, you can also see if the app is moving up or down in popularity. Like the app store, you may view the top apps in each different category, as well. While looking at reviews on any particular app, you not only can see what people are saying on iTunes, but also on various third-party websites. Through the app, it is also a breeze to mark whether you want the app or already own it.

No matter what class you teach, there will always be new apps available to purchase and download. Any of the apps already downloaded onto your device can have updates at any moment of the day. With the free AppShopper app, you can easily manage all of your current or future apps in one simple place.

Company: AppShoppper.com, LLC
Size: 4.7 MB
Rating: 4.5 Stars
Grade Level: All

6
Audioboo

Coming up with enough class projects that don't seem to be repeating themselves can become quite the task. Even if you change the topics, making slideshow after slideshow will lose its effect over time. Speeches consisting of standing up in front of the class and reading off of a note card can quickly become old, as well. If trying to start a new trend with projects, Audioboo can help get that started in app form.

Instead of having a group of students present a live report for the class, have them record it ahead of time with Audioboo. The app allows you to record your very own voice and play it back. An individual student or group of students can then pre-write a script and record it through a microphone onto the app. Allowing up to three minutes of recording time, any student can create their very own podcast of any kind to share with the class. Using Audioboo allows a student to record and rerecord their project to make sure it's perfect before sharing it with the class.

Besides using Audioboo for homework and assignments, it can also help a student perfect their speaking skills. If they're in the spring play, have them read their lines and record them. If they're in choir, they can record their singing. If they're in a speaking sport, they can record their speech. Even a band or orchestra could record the song they're learning. After recording their performance, the student or students can then listen to it. By hearing what they sound like, they can then know what others hear. They can pick out any mistakes and know where to fix them. If speech related, they can also determine if the point they wish to get across is evident or if they should add more emotion and inflection. By listening to their performance, it not only could help improve that specific one, but it could also help improve their skill for the future. They'll be identifying what they did wrong and will keep it in mind for future use.

On the same note, when a student or class records something, they can also share it with others. When these others listen to it, they, too, can comment on the performance and provide suggestions for the student. If they wish to publish the recording, they may also tag where they were when they recorded it, what it's about, and add a picture that is shown when it is being viewed. It can then be shared on social-networking sites and sent out via email.

The ability to speak well is a very important life skill, but there are more ways to learn the trait besides giving speeches. Sometimes hearing yourself speak or play an instrument and fine tuning from there is more beneficial in the end run. By using the free app, all grade levels can learn from the opportunities available with it. Whether it is used for homework, a project, or perfecting a speech, Audioboo can be a substantial learning lesson.

Company: BestBefore Media Ltd
Size: 6.2 MB
Rating: 3 Stars
Grade Level: All

7
AutoCAD WS

Every day, we go into a building. Not just a building, but multiple buildings. Most of the time, we take it for granted. We don't think about who designed it or how they did so. They seem as if they're there and always have been. However, upon thinking about it, we realize that this is not the truth and people were actually paid to design these things. Whether you're a basic middle school class teaching a variety of computer software programs or a high school course specializing in architecture, the CAD software is bound to come up. With AutoCAD WS, you can now learn about the software on your iPad.

By using AutoCAD WS, you can create and design your very own house or building. You can easily tap objects to select, move, or rotate them while creating your building. Drawing or editing shapes with accuracy is also a simple task when using Snap or Ortho modes. Through the app, you can add or edit text in the plan, which removes paper mark-ups. If you're drawing for an actual location, you can compare the distance of various parts when you're onsite.

While viewing your project, you can have it shown in both 2D and 3D modes. All of the layers, external references, and image underlays are also shown. By the use of multi-touch, you can also zoom and pan the image to navigate larger projects. If ever lost in your own drawing, you may also use GPS to determine where you are. When it comes to saving, all of your projects are saved online to your account for future reference and use. However, if you are not within Internet access, it is also an option to save a local version to your device until you have an Internet connection.

If you or a student wishes to share the drawing with anyone, AutoCAD WS provides a wide variety of options. All of your sharing can be done directly from your device. While working on a specific project with another person, two people may work on the file simultaneously. In real time, all edits on either end will immediately be realized and changed while you are connected to the Internet. Every one of your projects can be saved as a PDF or DWF and emailed to others. These people can then download the building and edit it on their own. If your device is enabled for it, you can also print the project directly from your app to your printer.

No matter how far in depth your class may go into the world of architecture, AutoCAD WS can teach a wide variety learning levels. If you only go into the basics, a class can easily take advantage of viewing a CAD program's capabilities. When dealing with a more advanced class, students can also learn and benefit from using a program which allows them to create and share a building of their very own. This free app is a must have for all computer or building and architecture-related classrooms.

Company: Autodesk
Size: 15.2 MB
Rating: 3.5 Stars
Grade Level: Middle-High School

8

Book Creator–eBook, PDF Creator

Is your class full of aspiring authors? Or do you have a graphics class that needs to work on page layout? How about a bunch of kindergarteners who want to be featured in their very own book? Whatever your situation may be, Book Creator is an app that can be put to use in any class of any grade level. Writing your own story just got more fun!

Instead of having every student type their paper and print it out, create your own digital classroom library! Through the Book Creator app, you and your class can make your very own books to read and share with each other. After writing and planning out your book, you can type it into your iPad. Anything's possible. You can make photo books, video books, art books, fairy tales, cookbooks, PR books, manuals, or PDF documents of your own. Let your imagination take control with the various amounts of layouts the app has to offer.

When creating your book, you can make it more than just text on a page. If you have photos saved into your devices library, you can easily incorporate them into your very own book. To make the picture exactly the way you want it, you can also move, enlarge, reduce, and rotate the image into the perfect position. You may also choose the quality of the image when you download it into the program. Depending on the content of your book or story, you may also add a video into its pages. All you have to do is select it from your library on your device. The pages that feature pictures or videos can also have text incorporated into them. The font, size, color, and placement of the text on your page can easily be edited to liking, as well. While building your book, the order of your pages can also be easily rotated throughout the entire process.

Once your book is created, it's time for you to share your masterpiece. By saving your creation in general eBook format, you can save your book onto the iBooks app. If you so desire, you can also register your books at the iBookstore for everyone to download. You may also email your book to students and their families. Book Creator also allows you to save your book in a PDF format. When saved in a PDF format, it can then be downloaded to your computer and eventually printed if you still want a hard copy.

For only $3.99, Book Creator can become the start of your new digital classroom library. However, instead of featuring the classics and all of today's modern stories, the entire spotlight can go to your very own students. When you have everyone's own stories saved into iBooks, every student can read and enjoy their classmates' creativity. It can be almost as if they've got their very own book or paper published. You can also share and save a class' artwork or class photographs for years to come.

Company: Life Lab
Size: 22.0 MB
Rating: 3 Stars
Grade Level: All

9
CloudOn

Every class within most recent years has required the use of MS Word, Excel, or PowerPoint. With CloudOn, all of these programs can now be used on your classroom iPad. To take things a step further, any document can be saved to Dropbox and then edited and finished at a later date, on another device. This means any projects and homework assignments can now be done on your device, without being required to be finished in the same place.

CloudOn allows creating and editing of any Word document, Excel spreadsheet, or PowerPoint presentation. To make things better, the layout is similar, if not identical, to the versions everyone is familiar with on the computer. This makes the creation of anything similar to the process we are already accustomed to. Not only are the appearances of the programs the same, but all the features match up, too. You can display, edit, or create charts in any of the programs. Other familiar features include formatting changes, spell check, the ability to insert comments, and many more. In Excel, you can also pivot tables and enter equations just as you would on a regular computer. If you're using PowerPoint, you can also edit transitions between slides and present the entire slideshow from the iPad itself.

Even with the aspect of having Microsoft programs on your iPad, a more important advantage to CloudOn is the access it has to other online document saving places. Besides just Dropbox, CloudOn also connects to Box and Drive. Through any of these accounts, you can take your already started document and open it on another device or a computer. This can be beneficial to any student who chooses to work on an assignment on your class' device. It means that they don't have to finish the entire project in one place, but can instead save it online and work on it other places—including home. You can also share your works via email, which is yet another way to send a project to work on at home.

Besides starting your own project, you can also open other documents. These documents can be downloaded from your Dropbox, Box, or Drive account or one you received from an email. Also included in the app are an Adobe Reader and a File Viewer, which allows you to open nearly any type of file. These include PDF, PSD, JPG, PNG, GIF, and many more. While editing or viewing any of these files, CloudOn also automatically saves as you work to avoid losing any changes.

Nearly any class will find a reason to use Word, Excel, or PowerPoint. The availability to use them on your iPad makes things even more convenient. You can go beyond only working on documents and students can use the iPad to present something to a smaller group of others, or you can save everyone's finished documents onto CloudOn and grade them at home. For a free download, CloudOn provides a wide variety of uses.

Company: CloudOn, Inc
Size: 4.4 MB
Rating: 4.5 stars
Grade Level: All

10
Coolibah–Digital Scrapbook

Every day, teachers are looking for a new project or a more original way to create a slideshow presentation. Most ways seem either too similar or too complex. However, unique is only one of many words that begin to describe the Coolibah program. Being a Digital Scrapbook, you can use your creativity and use this free app for more than just presentations. Any student can scrapbook pictures from the school year, projects they've done this year, or use it as a digital portfolio. The possibilities are endless!

For starters, your digital scrapbook can feature the pictures saved on your iPad. On any given page, you can move, size, and rotate all of the photos on your page. Another basic of Coolibah is the layouts and kits. The amount of layouts available creates endless options involving elements, frames, and text. The basic free app allows you to choose from 17 different sets. You can pick from more than 600 premium sets that only cost $.99. These sets vary from Le Diva, Rocker Chicks, Café Latte, and hundreds more.

To make your digital scrapbook even more personalized or specialized to a certain topic, you can change fonts, colors, and borders. Within the kits are backgrounds that you may choose to go behind any page. There are over 50 fonts to choose from and customize by size and color. Besides choosing your own colors, Coolibah also features SmartPalette, which helps select the color that would look best with your chosen background. You can also choose and arrange different borders and frames for pictures. To add even more effect to the photo, you may also add a drop shadow to really make it stand out. If you're overlapping various parts on each page, you may also control which element is forward and which is backward. When you save things, you can always go back and rearrange any page, if you so desire.

With the Coolibah app, you can create unlimited albums with unlimited pages. When you finally finish your creation, you can view it in a slideshow presentation. This presentation can be saved for the individual student, the class, or even a ceremony. You may also send the finished product. Without leaving the app, you or a student can post it on online websites, send it in an email, or send it via a text. If it's worth sharing, it's no hard task to get it out there!

Coolibah can be more than just a scrapbooking app for stay-at-home moms. It can be used in any classroom or school environment, as well. If you'd like to share photographs from a class field trip, you can make a digital scrapbook for everyone to see. You could create a scrapbook showcasing the art students have done over the year or years. Coolibah can help you create a truly unique picture slideshow for the end-of-the-class picnic or ceremony. Whatever your environment may be, if you have a need to make a state-of-the-art presentation, Coolibah is your must-have free app.

Company: Scott Means
Size: 15.6 MB
Rating: 3 Stars
Grade Level: All

11
Cramberry

Sometimes repeating things over and over is the only true way to drill facts and definitions into your brain. That's why we have math and vocabulary flashcards available to purchase in nearly every store. To make things even more specific to a class, blank notecards are purchased and then filled in by a teacher or student. This process not only takes time, but also money to buy pack after pack of notecards that are quickly thrown away after the unit is over. However, with the use of Cramberry on your iPad, studying involving notecards became easier and more price effective.

Making flashcards on Cramberry is a breeze. While creating your study cards, both sides are viewed on the screen of your iPad simultaneously. By tapping back and forth on either side of the white rectangle, you can type in the exact same words you'd normally hand write on a paper version. Whatever your use for note cards is (learning a new language, improving your vocabulary, or studying for a test), Cramberry can easily replace your original studying process. You can easily determine which side of the card is shown to you by reversing what text is typed onto what side.

Going beyond the creation of your own cards, Cramberry also has premade sets from which to choose. Through Cramberry.net, you may download over 1,000,000 other sets for free. These sets can be made by the site or uploaded by other students and teachers! If you sync your sets to their online site, you may also download them onto other devices. Other students, teachers, or classrooms can use your set for their own studying purposes!

While studying, Cramberry allows the same repetitive nature of normal flashcard studying. The app shows you one side of the card.

After saying your answer—in your head or aloud—you can tap the screen once more. This will show you or the studying student the other side of the card. If your answer was correct, you simply swipe your finger to the right. If wrong, swipe your finger to the left. For an even more unique studying session, the app also provides a matching game. When studying a new deck of cards, you can see both the front and back sides of multiple cards in the deck. By doing this, you and your students can quickly learn both sides of the cards.

Flashcards can be incorporated into any grade or class. All courses and units are bound to have vocabulary or something of the type that needs reviewing. Cramberry can be used in any classroom. An individual student can study a set of words or facts on their own. Two students can quiz each other back and forth. A small group of students may all review together. The entire class can look at the flashcard and take turns saying the answer. For $3.99, the amount of topics available is endless. By incorporating technology, any class can find studying more fun.

Company: Lateral Communications, Inc.
Size: 0.9 MB
Rating: 4.5 Stars
Grade Level: All

12

Demibooks Composer

Most classrooms have a solid divide when it comes to writing. Either a student loves the process, or they can't stand it. Some writing projects also involve drawing pictures to go along with the words. This is yet another make or break for most students. Demibooks Composer is exactly what you'd expect and more. Have students compose their very own stories and pictures in a way never before experienced. The interactive features within the app can allow every student to make their adventure one of a kind.

Demibooks Composer takes you beyond the two-dimensional world of normal storytelling. Through the app, you and your students can create a new, interactive story to share with everyone. By adding animation, images, text, sounds, movies, and visual effects, any story can come to life via your iPad. There's no need to understand any outside programming to make a story come to life.

The first step in the creation of your interactive book is choosing its orientation. Demibooks Composer allows for both portrait and landscape. After selecting other basic layout features, you can easily import images and audio clips into your book. These files can be downloaded from both your iPad and your computer. Text can be added and edited by various basic styles. While building pages, Demibooks Composer features grid lines that can help line and prefect the placement of every picture and object. To make navigation through the story simpler, each page can be named and managed from the bottom of the app. By clicking on the page at the bottom, you can open or reopen the page for editing. You may also add complex behaviors in the animations by using the Effects Editor. All animations use realistic physics. Programming can also prevent animations from running into each other or overlapping while on the page. To add more depth, music, sound effects, and spoken words can be added to every page. Video files supported include .mov, .mp4, .m4v, and .3gp. Throughout the process, you can preview any changes in the app directly on the iPad. You can also rearrange the order of all the animations of the page.

Once your student's creation is finished, there are many ways to share it. If another classroom has the Demibooks Composer app, they may view the completed product on their own iPad. The finished book can also be saved to any Dropbox account to be viewed on separate devices. Any story can also be published. For a small fee, the book can be sent to the app store for anyone to download.

With Demibooks Composer, technology just became even more fun. This free app incorporates animation and sound to any student's story. Seamless animation for all stories looks realistic. All animations can be controlled to the exact way a student imagined. By adding music, videos, and pictures, the story becomes more than just words. For younger students, it can be programmed to have stories read aloud to them as they follow along. Demibook Composer can make the line between love and hate for writing less defined.

Company: Demibooks Inc.
Size: 62.6 MB
Rating: 4 Stars
Grade Level: All

13
Dictionary.com

The skill of being able to use a dictionary is an important one. However, once the skill is mastered, the process of flipping through the entire dictionary can be a long, time consuming one—not to mention the number of dictionaries a room must have to provide for an entire class. With the Dictionary.com app, your original, hard cover, 50-pound dictionary has met its match. Of all the dictionary apps out there, Dictionary.com's is just as stellar as the online version, only this time portable.

Just like the online website, you can easily type in any word or words for which you or a student need a definition. Whether you're on or offline, the Dictionary.com app allows access to over two million words. Beyond your normal dictionary, you can easily click the button next to the word to switch over to a thesaurus. The thesaurus also includes the same two million-plus words. Back on the definition page, the app provides more than your casual list of five definitions and pronunciation key. With your volume turned up, you can have the word pronounced aloud. This can be used to help settle arguments over who says it right or simply tell you how it should be said during your or your student's speech. The page will also include the word's history and origin, along with example sentences.

If looking for a word that you can't find, Dictionary.com will assist you in all ways that an app can. It will provide spelling suggestions if your search is not finding any results. You can also easily look back into your search history to find the same word again. If, after searching for awhile, you still cannot find a particular word, you may use the voice recognition search. Speak the word that you are trying to look up, and the app will search its database for it. The free version comes with five initial voice searches, but you can cheaply add more through an in app purchase.

To make things more fun, Dictionary.com has even more entertaining features. Every day, the app provides a new word of the day. You can easily incorporate a new word of the day into any English or reading class. Students can write down these words in a notebook daily and even write sentences involving them, depending on how much time you're willing to spend with it. In the settings, you can also get the word of the day in a push notification. You can also add and favorite words. These can be fun and silly words or words that a student will need to complete a homework assignment. Adding them to your favorites can make the searching process easier and smoother. You may also shake the iPad for a random word to appear on the screen.

Instead of spending time paging through a dictionary, give the class a break. The free Dictionary.com app can be a simple tool for everyone to use. All ages can use the resource to look up words from an assignment, a book, or for a paper. The extra information and thesaurus also included make it a must-have learning and studying tool for everyone!

Company: Dictionary.com LLC
Size: 56.4 MB
Rating: 4.5 Stars
Grade Level: All

14
Doodle Buddy

Drawing using the computer seems like something for professionals and an overall foreign concept. People are slowly beginning to figure it out. With this, things are simplified. These simplified things can be perfect for fun or a true learning experience, depending on how you interpret it. Doodle Buddy is an app students may already be familiar with from their own devices or an older sibling. By incorporating it into day-to-day classroom use, students of all ages can get their turn at the classroom's iPad.

Saying Doodle Buddy is addictive can be an understatement. Painting, drawing, sketching, and scribbling all are an easy way to pass the time with this app. It's like finger painting, minus the mess. Students of any age will love the app. With over 44,000 different colors to choose from, you can feel like you're back in a kindergarten classroom. Doodle Buddy allows you to use multiple fingers at the same time. Many fun drawing tools include paintbrush, glitter, chalk, and smudges. If you ever mess up, you can undo your last mark or shake the entire iPad to start over. You can also apply stamps to your drawings. Each stamp incorporates a fun sound effect, as well.

Doodle Buddy can easily be a way to spend breaks. However, you can also integrate the app into a learning process. If you have a group of students in lower grades who are working with word families, use Doodle Buddy in a lesson. Instead of using paper, have them write out the new word families on the iPad. This will also help them continue working on spelling and formations of different letters. The app can also be used in spelling classes or to prepare for a spelling test.

Besides using the app for writing, math skills can be practiced on the Doodle Buddy app. Stamps can be a great place holder when it comes to math problems. The stamps can help with simple addition or subtraction problems. Students can put the 3 + 5 frog stamps on the page and then count them up for the final answer. For even more practice, they can write the original problem on the screen, as well. If you're in a more advanced grade dealing with multiplication, the same concept can also be used. This time, for 8 x 5, they can create eight groups of five stamps to help them visualize. A high school geometry class can even draw out their problems within the app to help them figure out the answers.

Outside of the fundamental classes, Doodle Buddy can be used in nearly any class. An art class can use the stamps and brushes to create their own projects. With the app, any student can express their artful side in a new way. Any finished products can also be emailed on to share with other classrooms, friends, or family.

To create a new learning process, Doodle Buddy can definitely do the trick. For free, classrooms filled with kids of all ages can learn and review. By using your imagination, new lessons plans can be fun and interactive for everyone. Not only can Doodle Buddy be a productive studying and learning app, but it can be tons of fun, too. For any free period, students can use it to draw and even play games, like hangman!

Company: Pinger, Inc.
Size: 12.8 MB
Rating: 3.5 Stars
Grade Level: All

15
Dragon Dictation

Sometimes you just can't remember how to spell a word. Sometimes you can't write down or understand what a person is saying because they talk too fast. Sometimes you have too many thoughts in your head and need a quick way to jot them down before you forget them. Worst of all is when one or all of these things happen and you don't have a way of solving them. Now, with the Dragon Dictation app, some of your woes and worries are quickly solved.

Basically, Dragon Dictation is a voice recognition app. Only this time, it's fast, simple, and extremely accurate. When opening the app, you are immediately met with a screen that says "Tap and Dictate." Below the words is a red button. It's as simple as that. Tap the button, begin speaking into your device's microphone, and it types every word you said. From here, you can begin using these typed words in your classroom.

One use of Dragon Dictation can be taken advantage of in any classroom environment, no matter the grade. Every student has a point where they can think of a word, but don't have any idea how to spell it. By using the app, the student can speak the word into the built-in microphone and then click "end." On the screen, the spelling of the word will appear, and they can easily copy it into their homework or assignment.

Another way of putting Dragon Dictation to use is while lecturing. In an upper grade level, long talks from the teacher are expected. However, sometimes a teacher will talk too fast, making it near impossible to write down every key note. If you record the lecture onto the app, students can then later look back at the entire lecture to pull out and copy down any notes and dates that they missed.

If a student is slow at typing or needs to get everything typed quickly, Dragon Dictation can do the job. Have them read the paper into the app. They'll have the paper finished in record speeds—up to five times faster than actual typing. Once typed, students can easily copy it out of the app and paste it into another one.

Besides just speaking to the app, you may also use it in reverse. After having Dragon Dictation type whatever you need it to, you can have it read back to you. This can help younger students with pronunciations of various words. For other practice, you can instead type in something and have it read it back to you that way, as well.

The unlimited ways of using Dragon Dictations can help in hundreds of situations. For free, the ability to have an app type everything for you is a must. All grade levels can find a use for this extremely accurate app. Students can easily use the app to brainstorm ideas and keep track of all the thought processes spinning in their heads. The ability to email and share your final works is just yet another advantage!

Company: Nuance Communications
Size: 7.7 MB
Rating: 3.5 Stars
Grade Level: All

16
Draw Something

Most drawing apps allow various drawings and are fun, but include no structure. They're a good way to waste time and have freeform drawing lessons, but generally tend to end there. Draw Something may be an app that many older students are already familiar with from their own at-home use. The app encourages out-of-the-box thinking, teamwork, and creativity in a much more structured manner.

Draw Something can be the start of something big at your school or in your classroom. By creating an account, you can share your username with other classrooms or iPads throughout the school. A one-on-one game between two usernames can be fun for everyone. You begin by picking from three words—each with a different difficulty and coin value. These words can vary from basic words, like sharks or golf, to pop culture terms and people, like Lady GaGa and Avengers. When it's your turn, you draw a picture of your selected word. Once finished, you send it to the opposing team, except for all purposes, they aren't exactly opposing. You must work together to draw a picture that the other can guess so you both can receive points. From a set of provided letters, the other person must type out what you drew. If it's right, you both get the coins for what the word was worth—one, two, or three coins. Coins can be saved up to buy more drawing colors. When a round is finished, the opposite team draws a picture for you to guess and things continue to rotate. If at any point you cannot determine the word from your given letters, you can use a bomb to destroy letters that are not featured in the word. Extra bombs can also be bought with collected coins. When out of bombs, you can pass on the word. By passing, neither team gets coins and the counter of how many turns in a row have taken place gets set back to one.

Unlike other basic drawing apps, Draw Something requires you to be creative while drawing your pictures. While pictures are being drawn, there is no timer and, therefore, no need to rush through the picture. Students can take their time and make sure everything is exactly how they pictured it. Through Draw Something, you can also tell a story to explain the word. Take the word "omelet," for example. First, you can draw an egg or carton of eggs. Then you can erase the picture and draw a bowl with a whisk. Eventually, you can draw a frying pan to get to the actual word "omelet." This process of storytelling is a great way of thinking outside of the box.

Once everyone with an iPad in your school downloads Draw Something for free, the fun can truly begin. Share everyone's usernames with each other in the school and have mini school competitions. See which two classrooms can have the highest running total of games or who can get the most coins. Students in classrooms of all ages can take turns being the drawing representative for the class during breaks. Everyone can let their creativity flow!

Company: OMGPOP, Inc.
Size: 14.0 MB
Rating: 4.5 Stars
Grade Level: All

17
Dropbox

It can be a hassle to keep track of work that is transported from home to school and back again. Flash drives can get lost. There are even many websites that you can save things onto, but there are so many to choose from, that it's sometimes hard to decide which one to use. Dropbox allows you to save files online and then access them via your app.

When downloading the app, you can easily create a new account or access an existing one. Dropbox lets you save photos, documents, and videos on their online storage. A free account can store up to 2 GB of memory, but it can be upgraded for a larger storage capacity. With your Dropbox account, every device that you have registered under your account name will have every photo, document, or video saved onto it. This includes computers, iPads, iPods, phones, and even their online website. It's the best way to keeps everything in one place.

Students can sign up for a free Dropbox account to keep track of all their documents and projects. They can access it from both school and home. Many apps on the iPad offer the ability to save to Dropbox. This means that if a student or group of students is working on a project or document on the class iPad, they can save it to their online account for work at home. There is no need to worry about saving it to a flash drive from the iPad.

You can also have videos or documents saved into a Dropbox account open on your iPad to share with the entire class. By adding anything saved online to your favorites, you can view it without an Internet connection. If you have something you want to take on a field trip or any other out-of-school adventure, the Dropbox app is the way to go.

One of the things you can save onto your account can be a PDF. As eBooks become more and more popular, they become easier and easier to get a hold of in PDF format. While your class is reading a book and you have it saved in a PDF format, it can then be downloaded and saved into your iPad for the students to read.

All grade levels can use the simple way of transporting files that Dropbox provides. As a teacher, you can even save students' work to take home and grade via your account. If students wish to share files with their partners, they can send them by email and sign in and out of the app. This free app is a must have for document transporting and sharing.

Company: Dropbox, Inc.
Size: 9.8 MB
Rating: 4 Stars
Grade Level: All

18

eClicker Presenter, eClicker Audience

Students zone out. It's a well known fact. Sometimes it's hard to determine if they're truly zoning out or are actually grasping the information. Sure, quizzes and tests can tell you how many students got it, but those are way at the end of any unit. By using the eClicker apps, you can ask students questions throughout any lecture and get immediate feedback on their knowledge without any expensive equipment. The eClicker apps include a set of two different programs: eClicker Presenter and eClicker Audience. The two are compatible and work hand in hand with each other.

Teachers start the process with the eClicker Presenter app. On any device, you can make your questions ahead of time. You can make these questions in a variety of different types. This includes multiple choice, true/false, and agree/disagree. To add even more to any question, you may also incorporate pictures. If other teachers have created question sets, they can share them with you, as well.

From the eClicker Presenter app, you can control when the questions are available. Questions can be sent one at a time to fit along with the speed of your presentation or all at the same time. That could allow students to answer them at their own pace, as well as let them read through them ahead of time. You can get instant reports after each talk and save the results to check the progress over time. By seeing these results, it can be easy to determine which questions students are struggling with and what needs to be reviewed.

On the students' end, they will be able to download their app for free. They can sign in on the eClicker Audience app on any device, whether it is their own iPod touch or a classroom iPad. They may also sign in from the Internet or a smart phone. eClicker Presenter for the iPad can hold 64 participants, and the iPhone version handles 32. Either one is enough to allow for an entire class.

Students' devices will recognize your app's signal. After clicking on it, they can then sign in with their name and an optional username. The questions that you created are then shown on their screen at the speed you predetermined. Any picture that you added to a question is also displayed on their device. This eliminates the hassle of not being able to see the picture or diagram from a projector. After the presentation, the students immediately get the results of the quiz. They can view the questions they got wrong.

These two sets of apps can be incorporated into a class of any level. First graders can answer math facts, and biology students can answer the function of various cell structures. Not only does it encourage students to pay attention during lectures, but it also makes it more fun and allows you to track your class' progress. You can even use the agree/disagree questions to take opinions or use it while presenting an idea to coworkers. These apps could also be incorporated with after-school extracurricular activities and programs. eClicker Presenter and eClicker Audience are a win for everyone.

Company: Big Nerd Ranch, Inc.
Size: 3.4 MB, 1.0 MB
Rating: 4.5 Stars, 4 Stars
Grade Level: All

19
Edmodo

Social networking sites are something that has become part of our day-to-day life. Many people, students and teachers included, have already jumped on the bandwagon. These sites could easily be used to keep track of daily assignments and long-term projects, but, unfortunately, many are not willing to keep it strictly school related. Edmodo is an online website built much like these social networking sites, only it's made specifically for schools. With the Edmodo app, you and students can access the site through any mobile device.

With a layout similar to that of Facebook, every student can make their very own Edmodo account. With Edmodo, students can view and turn in assignments and check their most recent grades. Teachers can post alerts to an entire class, check who has what assignment turned in, and grade assignments. Class discussions are easy to have with the Edmodo app, both during and after school hours.

Every student and teacher may create a profile page. Through the profile pages, students may post back and forth between their teachers and other classmates. This creates an environment that allows students to easily ask questions, even when they are at home. Other students and teachers may help them through their problem. Edmodo also allows people to create groups to separate between various classes and after-school activities or sports.

Another feature with Edmodo is the ability to assign, complete, and submit homework. As a teacher, you can create the assignment and post a due date. Your students may then complete it online or within the app. When they begin to turn it in, you may start grading them and post the grade for only the student to see. Since all of your students will get the document linked directly to them, you won't have to deal with any more excuses involving not getting it. Students may also check their past grades with the built-in grade book. If there are any questions or concerns involving a grade, a student can easily message you to get it fixed as soon as possible. Edmodo also features a calendar to keep track of meetings, due dates, and trips.

There are many ways you can use Edmodo in any classroom. It makes communication with your students a much easier process. For any assignments that require links to other websites, you can easily post them for everyone. You can send encouragement or reminders to any student via a post or message. If they had a review packet for a test the next day, you can send them the answers later in the night for comparison purposes. Your classroom can even create a co-classroom from anywhere around the world. Edmodo is also a great way to stay organized. You can post a schedule for students each day to keep everyone on the same page.

This free app allows everyone to have easy access to each other. Edmodo is a great way to keep everyone organized and on the same page. The ability to take it with you on any device is perfect for everyone.

Company: FushionProjects, Inc
Size: 6.6 MB
Rating: 2.5 Stars
Grade Level: Middle – High School

20
Educreations Interactive Whiteboard

Drawing apps are nothing new to the iPad, and Educreations Interactive Whiteboard is in no way, shape, or form the first one. It is instead one of the few specifically directed toward classrooms. You can now create your very own video lessons to share with students in and out of the classroom. It's truly the new and improved whiteboard of the future.

Educreations Interactive Whiteboard features 10 colors to create your very own new lesson or review. You start by hitting "record." Next, everything that you draw or write on the page is recorded and saved to the video you will end up creating. You can easily pause and resume recording at any point. To help you more, you may insert pictures onto the whiteboard screen from your iPad camera, a photo album, or a Dropbox account. These pictures may be drawn on top of, animated, and drug around to help you further explain everything. You may also create multiple whiteboard pages in one video. To add even more, you can provide a verbal description through a microphone and record your voice into the video. If at any point you make a mistake, with the click of a button, you can undo and redo anything. By making a free online account, you can upload all of your lessons to their website. You may also control who is capable of viewing these videos. Your lessons can also be emailed or uploaded onto your website and blog.

The ways that Educreations Interactive Whiteboard can be incorporated into a learning environment are endless. You can record an example of the day's math problem and post it. Students can watch the video as a review of the process or to answer any questions. If a student was sick, they may also use the video to help make up for the class they missed during their absence. Putting the lesson online before class is another option. This will allow students to learn it before class and ask questions before completing their homework assignments. You can also label parts of a diagram for any class to provide further explanation. Educreations Interactive Whiteboard can also let you tutor someone from afar or outside of the school day. By emailing a student a video, they can learn the day's material before the next class. If you coach a sport, you can even map out plays before the big game and share it with the entire team.

With Educreations Interactive Whiteboard, students will be able to learn and relearn every lesson that has ever caused them grief. Once you download your finished video to your website or the Internet, students may it as a resource for explanations and information on nearly anything. They can watch and rewatch what you've taught them at home. They can also watch any video on the classroom's iPad during a study hall or any other break. To make things even better, all of Educreations Interactive Whiteboard's features are entirely free.

Company: Educreations, Inc.
Size: 2.5 MB
Rating: 4.5 Stars
Grade Level: All

21
EMD PTE (Periodic Table)

In most science-related classrooms, periodic tables are something that you always have sent down to the office to be copied. They are commonly used and also commonly lost or thrown away—hence the extra copies. Most of the time, they aren't even intricate copies—just the basic atomic number, element abbreviation, mass, and maybe a few other parts. By getting the EMD PTE app, not only will you no longer be wasting paper copies of this key tool to the science world, but you'll get more information than one can fit on an individual sheet of paper.

The basic look of the periodic table in the EMD PTE app makes it look not only vibrantly colored, but also very straightforward. Each brightly colored area nicely divides every group of elements into their similar groupings. By clicking on any element, more information than you thought possible will appear. A simplified version will show the atomic number, abbreviation, full name, classification, the group and period it lies in, and the atomic mass. For a more in-depth version, you can also see more individual groups, like if it's natural, artificial, or radioactive, along with its history. In fact, you can even view the entire periodic table by the pictures of the discoverers. The app also provides the state it is at room temperature, the year of discovery, melting and boiling point, appearance, and other specific atomic properties. Some elements even have a picture. If you would like to organize all of the elements, you can easily order them in almost any matter. You can list them by their number, density, electronegativity, and many other features. Yet another very helpful feature is the ability to type in various chemical formulas. The EMD PTE app will tell you the mass of the equation, along with what percent each element takes up in the composition.

This app version of the periodic table is a great tool for both students and teachers. Teachers in all areas of science can use it to plan lessons and assignments. They may even use it to get the answers for the homework they assign. Students can use the EMD PTE app to help them through any assignment. They can also use it to study for an exam or for just plain fun. If you only have one iPad in the classroom, everyone will be able to share the wonderfulness of the app. If everyone has their own, they can easily use it for their day-to-day work and assignments.

To easily rid your class of paper waste, downloading an app version of the periodic table is a must. Sure, any app may do, but if you want more than just a picture, EMD PTE is your way to go. With this app, teachers and students alike can not only learn more than they thought imaginable about the periodic table, but enjoy doing so. The many different features and facts the app offers is something that every science classroom must have. And it may even inspire some of our future chemists.

Company: EMD Chemicals
Size: 8.2 MB
Rating: 4 Stars
Grade Level: Middle – High School

22
Evernote

Organization. It's always been something that many have had a hard time keeping track of or managing. Whether it's short-term or long-term, it's a concept you either grasp or you don't. If you don't, the first step to solving the problem is accepting it. The next is downloading Evernote. Both teachers and students can use Evernote to keep track of their projects, assignments, ideas, and so much more.

Evernote allows you to create and edit notes, to-do lists, and task lists. You can also save, sink, and share files. These files include documents, videos, voice-recordings, and pictures. This means that if you find it easier to say what you're thinking than typing it, you can easily record it directly into the app. Any of the things saved into your account can also be accessed on any other device, the Internet, or saved onto your desktop. It will even connect to other apps you have on your iPad. A key zinger for Evernote is the means that it uses to organize all of your various notes. For starters, everything can be divided into different "notebooks"—or folders. However you decide to label these notebooks is entirely up to you or your students. You can make a notebook for each separate class or for each unit. To subdivide these notebooks even further, you can also add tags to any note. This allows you to get very exact and very organized. Any notes or notebooks can be shared with anyone.

By using Evernote in the classroom, you can keep everyone on top of things. For teachers, you can easily keep track of all your classes on a day-to-day or week-to-week basis. If know something that can be used for an upcoming unit on the presidents, you can easily tag the note as #presidents. All other ideas for this same unit would then be put under that same tag to keep them together. As other units come along, you can create them a tag of their own. During a break, if you were to go to a conference of some sort, you could tag any and every bit of useful information you learned there into the app, as well. If you keep track of all your lesson plans ahead of time via Evernote, you can easily send them along to a sub if you are sick. During class, you can have easy access to all of the day's handouts and send any extra notes to students. By taking a picture of the whiteboard with notes on it, you can even send it to an absent student.

For students, Evernote can be the ideal studying tool. They can easily type the day's notes into the app and send it to any other device they may have. By doing this, they will be able to go paperless and not have to worry about losing any of their note sheets. However, if they do prefer to handwrite their notes, they can take a picture of them and save them into the app, just like they would with the typed version. This picture-taking concept can also be used for textbooks. Instead of lugging home a 50-pound textbook, students can take a picture of the needed pages and go from there. If there is a very important lecture or lesson at any point, they can easily record it and listen to it later, as well. The notebook and tagging system can also help them keep track of their different classes, activities, and research.

As a free app, Evernote is the way to go when it comes to organization. Both students and teachers can use it to stay on top of their busy lives and multiple classes. By using it on your class iPad, everyone can benefit.

Company: Evernote
Size: 19.4 MB
Rating: 4.5 Stars
Grade Level: Middle – High School

23
Explain Everything

As technology improves, presentations are getting more and more fun by the day. The good ol' writing on the whiteboard is quickly being replaced with the newest advancements in technology. If you have used, or plan on using, an iPad in your classroom and are considering getting into this new manner of presentations, then the Explain Everything app is a must.

Creating explanations, presentations, and tutorials just got more fun. Explain Everything is easy to use and allows you to do a wide variety of things to any presentation. You can explain and animate nearly any topic. By recording drawings from on screen, you can email them or even add them to the Internet directly from the app. This means no uploading it to their website and then your own. Explain Everything also allows you to upload any finished video onto other websites, like Dropbox and Evernote. Along with just drawing or writing into the app, you can also upload many other documents. You can upload images (from both the iPad's camera and the saved library), PDFs, PowerPoints (from that day's lessons), Excel Spreadsheets, documents and also anything out of your Dropbox or Evernote account. Recorded sounds and descriptions from the iPad's microphone can also be added. All of the things you create with the app—whether they are videos, pictures, or PDFs— can be exported to others for viewing and editing. You can even tape things and have them streamed live online as you do them.

Explain Everything is the perfect way for teachers to help and explain everything to students who have questions. You can easily post it onto your website to explain the process of a math problem, the locations on a map, or almost anything you can think up. To incorporate the Explain Everything app into the actual class day, you can use it to test students. You can set them up into groups and have a predetermined problem for them to solve. If you are working on ordering fractions from least to greatest, you can give students a set of predetermined fractions. They can then record all their work as they figure out their order and move them around on the screen. By recording this, you can go back and watch their entire process and see where they may need help. If you only have one iPad, then students can take turns. If you're in an environment with multiple iPads, everyone can do it at the same time.

Students can also use the Explain Everything app to help their fellow classmates. If any student cannot get in contact with you outside of school and one of their classmates has the app, they can ask them for help. The student who understands the work or problem can record it into the app. They can then email it to their classmate.

The professionalism of every video explanation that comes out of the Explain Everything app is something everyone should have. Both students and teachers will benefit from its existence. For only $2.99, this specifically-made-for-the-classroom app is a must have.

Company: MorrisCooke
Size: 8.6 MB
Rating: 4 Stars
Grade Level: All

24
Flashcard*

You've heard it a hundred times before, and you're about to hear yet again. Flashcards. They're arguably the best way to get facts stored into your brain. Their repetitive nature can take studying to new places. As these simple things slowly begin to advance themselves with technology, they become more and more convenient to the general population. By downloading Flashcard*, you will be doing both you and your students a favor.

Like most flashcard apps out there, Flashcard* allows you to create your own flashcards and download premade sets from the Internet. Flashcard* uses the website Quizlet for your downloading of any deck. If you are downloading a deck with hundreds of cards, you don't have to wait for all of them to be saved into the app. You can start with the front of the deck and work on the already finished ones. These longer decks, whether you downloaded them or made them yourself, are easily supported and don't cause any glitches or slowness. By creating the cards in Flashcard*, you can give up dealing with hard-to-read handwritten ones. To make these flashcard decks even more impressive, you can even download pictures to help you study. If at any point you wish to edit a deck, you can go back and do so. This includes both the cards that you made and the ones you downloaded from Quizlet. While studying, you can flip through the deck at any speed you want. You can also view the cards in portrait and landscape. For any cards you're having problems with, you can mark them to come back to or remove the ones you already know. Flashcard* also allows you to study them in any order—random, alphabetically, or one that you choose.

How to use flashcards for studying is practically common knowledge. By having all of your decks saved onto your iPad, you no longer have to worry about carrying around the stack or losing one of the cards. If you only have one iPad, students can use the app to study between classes, during a break, or after they are done with all of their work. If there are more iPads available, then even more people have it available for their own use. Multiple students can even group up to study and review.

If students use the Flashcards* app on their own, they will have even more opportunities to take advantage of its features. They can easily take it home with them and use all of their decks without an Internet connection. Flashcards* also lets students email their decks to other people, like classmates, for their own uses. The decks can also be saved onto Dropbox and shared that way.

There are many flashcard apps out there for people to download. Most of the time, it generally comes down to personal preference. However, one of the key features of Flashcards* is its ability to download pictures. This can help you study parts of things – like a cell – or a map. Students, teachers, and classrooms of all levels can make use of this free app.

Company: Jeffery Holliday
Size: 2.7 MB
Rating: 4.5 Stars
Grade Level: All

25
Flashcards+

Whether you're studying states and capitals, vocabulary and definitions, or a new language, Flashcards+ is a must-have app for your classroom. Flashcards have always been integrated into a system that requires memorizations of facts and definitions. With it now available in app form, it becomes even more convenient. When using Flashcards+, the concept of actually spending money toward buying notecards is gone. The many different topic choices and features make it a vital app for any classroom.

One of the most beneficial aspects to the Flashcards+ app is the wide variety of premade flashcard sets there are available to download for free. It links to the online website Quizlet.com, which opens you up to over 8.5 million different sets. Nearly every topic you could ever imagine is available to download onto your very own app for free. With these sets premade, it removes the time needed to make any of the actual notecards, and thus creates more time for actual studying! However, if the exact topic you require is not available or not exactly what you desired, you can also make a set of notecards of your very own, fitting your own classroom needs. This means that you can personalize each deck to your exact unit, in your exact subject.

Among the vast majority of decks you can choose from or create yourself, there are even more features that make this basic studying app a necessity. One of the most helpful is the option to check the flashcards that you already know with a check mark. This allows you to go back and review only the cards that you have not yet accomplished while studying. You may also search through each deck for one specific card. When it comes to shuffling or reshuffling, you only need to shake the device to scramble the deck. While studying, you can also switch which side of the card you would like to view at any time. So if you want to start studying the definitions, and then eventually graduate up to viewing just the word, it is merely a settings change and classroom. The app also works in either horizontal or vertical orientation, depending on your preferences and the way you not a whole new deck change. On every deck, you may additionally change font size to fit your need, whether it is nearby viewing or across the hold your device.

Yet another convenient feature is the many different languages the app has to offer. With 22 languages supported, it can make the app fun and educational for many situations, especially a language classroom. These different languages offer the possibility of having each card read aloud to the student or class. On top of that, by in-app purchase, you may also buy various dialects and genders to read each card. These different accents can bring even more fun into the entire studying process!

While keeping the same classic look of 3 by 5 notecards we all know so well, Flashcards+ is able to incorporate fun studying habits and modern technology to the fullest. With endless options of topics and overall features that make each deck your very own, the app is a true need for any classroom, regardless the age or subject. Ridding of the paper waste of old flashcards, this free, ad-less app is one that anyone can apply to their daily need.

Company: Connor Zwick
Size: 9.9 MB
Rating: 4.5 Stars
Grade Level: All

26
FotoBabble

Sometimes coming up with new ways to expand creativity in a student's mind can be quite the task. Even coming up with a new assignment or way of teaching can be taxing. A way to show a student's capability is by testing their knowledge on the spot. With the use of FotoBabble, you can do just that.

The basic process of using FotoBabble is a simple one. They like to claim three simple steps: taking or picking a photo, adding voice and enhancing the photo, and sharing it with others. While selecting your photo, it can be one out of your library or one that you take directly from your iPad. The next part is where most of the work is actually done. You can record and rerecord your voice to be saved with the picture. This recording can be of you explaining something, a speech, or just the everyday background buzz of the classroom. FotoBabble also allows you to add effects, colors, and borders to the picture. After everything is finished, you can both save the video and email it to other people.

Although Fotobabble may seem like an app that can only be used with social networking sites, classes of all levels can find a use for it. For elementary students, they can use it for vocabulary learning. Younger elementary students can have a picture shown to them from their vocabulary list, and they can then record themselves saying it. You can save this to check later. Older elementary students can find their own picture, say the vocabulary word, and also recite the definition. After learning the words this way, you can use it as their final "test" or test them later with a hard copy.

Students in middle or high school who are learning a foreign language can also use FotoBabble. You can have each student take a picture of whatever the word or phrase is or is referring to, or even the picture of the words on the board. They can then record themselves saying the word or phrase into the app in the language they are learning. You can use this recording to help you grade their pronunciation. Students can also use their classmates' videos to learn or study their various words.

Fotobabble can also be used in elective classes. A class of art students preparing for an art fair can easily make use of the app. They can take a picture of their art piece and record themselves explaining it for everyone at the fair to hear. Gym and Phy-Ed classes can use it to help explain various procedures they are learning. Sports teams can use it in the same way.

The many ways of using Fotobabble in your classroom are endless. All of the different things you have students record can also be used to show parents at teacher conferences. For a free app, Fotobabble is a must have for classrooms of all levels.

Company: Fotobabble, Inc.
Size: 6.3 MB
Rating: 3 Stars
Grade Level: All

27
Free Books – 23,469 Classics to Go

As people convert over to digital copies of books, it seems we tend to be re-buying the books we already own. It'd be nice if we could get some of these books for free, especially the classics that we've learn to love so much. That's exactly what the Free Books app does. It provides exactly what its title suggests it does: 23,469 of our classic pieces of literature available to download and take with us anywhere—all for free.

The amount of books the app gives you for free is quite obvious, and it's safe to say it's a lot. These books can vary from letters from leaders and autobiographies of people like Benjamin Franklin and Andrew Carnegie, to classic Victorian Age writings and Shakespeare. Since most of these books are in the public domain, it's almost guaranteed that if you can think of it, it's there. You can easily download any of these books onto your iPad, even the audio book for some. If you have other books bought for a different eReader device, they can also be saved into the app for you to read. Just like other eReaders, the Free Books app also features things like taking notes, highlighting certain suggestions, bookmarking pages, and a built-in dictionary. It also recommends books suggestions for you, has high quality book covers, let's you email them to your computer, and even has a night-time reading mode.

By downloading the Free Books app, everyone is in a winning situation. Younger students are sure to find a book of their level, and the same thing goes for older students. Free Books can be used for actual required reading or just for fun and curiosity. If there is only one iPad available to use in the classroom, you can even read a book to the class directly from the iPad or play them the audio book, if it is available. Students can also use it in a study hall to read anything they want. If there are multiple iPads available, everyone can read the book they are currently learning about in class on their own app.

23,469 is a big number. It's also a lot of books, and more are added with each update. Of all the eBook-related apps available, you really can't get much better than the Free Books app. As students begin to read more of the classics, they'll all become that much more informed Some students may even surprise you..

Company: Spreadsong, Inc
Size: 42.7 MB
Rating: 4.5 Stars
Grade Levels: All

28
GeoMaster Plus HD

Geography can be and is studied at many different levels. Elementary students can learn states and capitals. Students in middle school can learn the countries. Older students can continue this study of the countries and learn cities, too. The geography of our earth isn't going anywhere anytime soon. It's important that we know and learn it. The GeoMaster Plus app is a perfect way of doing this. If you already know these things, then it can be an easy source of fun.

GeoMaster Plus features a very detailed atlas. Here you can search for any country and view its location. All of its maps are also of a very high resolution. However, the app is so much more than your simple type-in-the-search-box atlas. What really makes GeoMaster fun is its quizzes. There are more than 40 different difficulty levels for you to work through. The quizzes can vary from general knowledge, to things that will take you many rounds to get the hang of. Some possible categories are world capitals, European countries, Asian countries, African countries, South American countries, U.S. cities, U.S. states, and French departments. There is even a flag version in the works! All quizzes are timed to ensure that you really do know your stuff. Whatever your knowledge level may be, there are many things to learn and enjoy from GeoMaster.

Students of all ages can use GeoMaster Plus to their advantage. Elementary students who are figuring out the location of things for the first time can use it to test their skills. The United States quiz is a great way for them to prepare for an upcoming test. They can even practice learning their state capitals.

Students in middle and high school can use the more advanced quizzes. Using the timer, they can test the quick reflexes for countries, cities, and even Chinese provinces. GeoMaster can be used to study for a test, to learn, or just have fun. The more time students spend on the app, the more they'll know and the more impressed their friends and family will be. Some may not even notice all the knowledge they are gaining from this additive app.

Whether you're looking to study or have app for only $3.99. Who knows, just have fun, GeoMaster is a must- after downloading it, you may be hosting after-school tournaments to see which students knows the most. You may even have teachers eager to join in on the fun. It is a fun way to pass the time and learn while you're at it.

Company: Visuamobile
Size: 167 MB
Rating: 4.5 Stars
Grade Level: All

29
Google Search

When starting a research project or looking for the answer to a question, it seems our first and foremost place to look is Google, and it's the truth. There are many other search engines out there, but most people tend to lean toward Google, if not only for its popularity. Now, instead of going all the way to the computer to type in what you need, you can do it directly from the Google Search app on your iPad. It doesn't even require opening Safari.

The Google Search app features many of your favorite things you can use on the computer version. You can search the web, images, videos, news, and every other tab available on the computer. When you show images and websites, you can view them as a list and icons, like normal, or sweep through them with full page previews. While searching, you will also get your word or phrase suggestions just like you do online. On the main page of the app, you can also view your past searches to make things easier and quicker to find. Another feature and new way of searching is with voice recognition. If typing isn't fast enough or just isn't your thing, you can say what you'd like to search into the microphone. The app will type in what you say and search for you that way. On any page, you can also use the "find" feature. This allows you to search for a word or phrase on a site you have open. Any page that you find can easily be shared via email right out of the app. You can also easily access other Google apps, like Gmail, Docs, Calendar, and Translate. The Google app also features the Google Goggles. These allow you to take a picture of what you want to learn about, and it will do the search from there. By using "search nearby," the app will show you results that are relevant to where you are.

92 Amazing Apps for Teachers

Some of the uses for Google are quite obvious. Students of all ages can use it to research and find answers to any questions that they have. They can also find pictures and look at maps and videos. You can even use it for your own work to help create assignments or find websites to do web quests on. Most of these concepts are pretty self-explanatory. However, a major thing that can be taken out of the Google Search app is the Google Goggles. If you are out with the class, like on a field trip, you can take a picture of any monument you come across. The app will then search for you and brings up even more information. You can even use this feature to help solve Sudoku problems.

Everyone uses Google, and on a day-to-day basis for most. By having the Google app of the iPad, you won't need to find a computer to search for one little thing. Students can easily use the iPad to search for their answer. If every student or group of students has their own iPad, you can even spend entire work days for a research project in the classroom. All of the information can be found on the Google Search app. For a free app, you're not going to find something else that everyone in the class enjoys and knows so well.

Company: Google Mobile
Size: 14.2
Rating: 4.5 Stars
Grade Level: All

30
GrooveMaker Free for iPad

Tracks. Grooves. Beats. When all these words are separate, they can all have their own completely different meaning. However, when talking music, any type of song or album wouldn't get very far without the three of them. Without beats, you wouldn't have grooves of the song. Without grooves, you wouldn't have a track. Without tracks, you'd have no album with songs. It's these three aspects that GooveMaker Free likes to focus in on. With this app, you can have your own professional sounding songs made to your liking and need.

GrooveMaker Free includes 120 loops and 8 tracks. You can use these to make limitless amounts of different tracks in your app. While making your "groove," you won't have to pause it at any time since it is done in real time. The app allows many different features to make each track truly your own. You can pick a drum rhythm. You can add a string of bass notes. You can add the beat of a bass drum. These basic musical aspects are only the start of your creation. To add more originality, you can also add various melodies, lead instruments, background harmonies, or effect loops. The tempo of your piece can be sped up or slowed down at any time during your recording. Other features like solo and mute can all be accessed from the same screen. Your loops can be edited and your grooves can be switched, all by a simple tap on the screen. The grooves you make can be dragged into any order that you want. All of your finished tracks can be saved and downloaded as a WAV file onto to your computer.

The process of creating these grooves is a great learning experience. It also allows the creativity juices to flow. Younger students can use it to have fun and maybe even learn what sounds good together and what doesn't. Students in higher grade levels can also use it as a learning process and as a way to express themselves. If they are planning to go into a music-related career, GrooveMaker Free is a great way to help them prepare for their future. They can figure out different rhythms and create their own tracks. Some people also have a constant original melody in their head. These students can use the app to put these rhythms into an actual song.

Any saved track or song can also be saved for other classroom or school use. Students can make their own songs for use in their projects. If they are making a video or movie for any class, GrooveMaker Free can help them create background music. The music you make in the app can also be used at dances for students to show off to all of their peers.

The amount of different tracks you can create with GrooveMaker Free is limitless. Everything in the app is easy to catch on to and appealing to the eye. Professional sounding tracks for any and everything will become the norm. Almost any musical groove can be easily created, and all at your fingertips and iPad.

Company: IK Multimedia US, LLC
Size: 12.3 MB
Rating: 3.5 Stars
Grade Level: Middle – High School

31
Groupboard

The more we see apps coming out for day-to-day uses, the more we see them improving our lives. Some of the most helpful ones improve collaboration. Groupboard is a free app that lets you do exactly that. You can easily draw, chat, and collaborate with students and other teachers.

Everything done on Groupboard is done in real time. You can collaborate with other people who have an iPod, iPad, or even just good ol' internet connection. If they wish to get in on the conversation, all they need is an Internet conversation. With the free edition, up to five people can sign into any one board. For more people to join, you'll have to pay for a subscription. While writing in the app, you can use multiple colors, along with being able to change the line thickness. There is a picture in the bottom of an eraser to help remove any mistakes. To get rid of everything on the page, you can also shake the iPad. Pinching in with two fingers can allow you to zoom in on the page and scroll to get a better look at things that people have written. Groupboard also has various tools that you can use. If you wish to add a picture to your conversation, you can download one from your library or take a picture of something. You can then write on top of the picture to help point things out. To download documents into it, you'd have to pay for a subscription, but it is still a possibility. The iPad version also allows you to print an image from your screen. Previous Groupboards that you have used can be saved in your settings, and you can easily search for others directly in the app.

The greatest aspect of Groupboard is the ability to work together on anything. Most other whiteboard apps allow one person to create a video and then share it. By using Groupboard, everyone can get what they think is necessary to say out there. Sports teams can use the app to plan tactics together, without even having to be near each other. Students and teachers can also use it to tutor others in nearly any subject. For math, they can easily work together to solve a homework or example problem. Students can also use it to test themselves with spelling words or other facts by using the voice feature. They can speak to each other and write or draw the answer on the screen to check. Groupboard doesn't always have to be used with other people. An individual student can also use it as a reusable sheet of paper for homework.

If you require collaboration in your classroom between yourself and your students or your students with each other, Groupboard is your go-to app. Projects can be finished quicker and more efficiently. Studying from home will become easier. For a free app, you can't lose anything by downloading it for your iPad. In fact, you may actually benefit from it.

Company: Group Technologies Inc
Size: 0.9 MB
Rating: 2.5 Stars
Grade Level: Middle – High School

32
iBooks®

Reading on an electronic device is obviously getting more popular. There are bunches of different reading devices that have their own apps available through iTunes—not to mention the other reading apps that are available to purchase on their own. The decision to determine which you one you'll choose to use may be a tough one. To make things easier, why not go with the app specifically designed by Apple® for their own device? iBooks is the way to go while reading books off of your iPad.

Many of the features that iBooks has available are designed specifically for the iPad by the ones who know it best. All of your classroom's favorite books can easily be purchased through the same account you use for iTunes. Besides normal books, iBooks also allows you to purchase interactive books, picture books, and even some textbooks. Other things that iBooks includes are free samples of the books before purchasing, the ability to reorder books you purchase, change the brightness of your screen, font, and font size, and so many other things. iBooks even allows you to change the color of pages from white, sepia, or white on black for night-time reading. You can bookmark your progress in any book and open up the same book, on the same page, on a different device. You can also leave notes when you bookmark your favorite parts of any story when you go back to reread it. There is a page navigator at the bottom of every page to provide an easy way to find different pages. Through iBooks, you can also download and read PDFs. These PDFs can also be printed from your device.

Students of all grades have to read books of some sort during the year. As a basic use, students can download any of the books they are reading onto their devices, both at school and at home. Through the iBooks apps, they can also bookmark and highlight parts they don't understand or want to comment on. Using the notes feature, they can add a reminder to themselves about their question or comment. If there is only one iPad for the class to use, then students can use it to read a book in their spare time. Many of the classics are available to download for free through the iBookstore®. This is a great way for students to experience the world of some of the greatest pieces of literature ever written.

Another way students can use iBooks is as a way to sample books. Before they read a book, they can download the sample onto the iPad. This gives them a taste of what to expect before they read the actual book. They can also use this to help them determine how much they want the book. By knowing what it'll be like, students can either buy the book on their iPad or in a hard copy to read again and again, or wait to get it from the library.

iBooks can easily inspire more students to read. The ability to read a long book without having to actually carry it around can be a huge advantage. Even if people only use it to preview books, this free app can be a new classroom favorite.

Company: Apple Inc
Size: 42.4 MB
Rating: 4 Stars
Grade Level: All

33
Idea Sketch

Lots of people get ideas on how to do various things, especially students. These ideas can include a story plot, facts to a research project or paper, and so many other things. The hard part isn't coming up with the ideas, but instead figuring out how to organize them. For some people, the best way of doing this is via flowchart or outline. Now, instead of doing it on a computer or hand writing it, you can download Idea Sketch and do it directly from your iPad.

Whatever you want to call it—a mind map, a concept map, a flowchart—you can easily create it with the Idea Sketch. The app is easy to catch on to and use. By typing your words into any word bubble and dragging it to where you want it to be placed, you can easily create your own diagram. You can also change the shape and color of each bubble. After creating the diagram, you can switch views and have an outline completely created and finished. Idea Sketch will create the whole thing for you as you work. This process can also be done in reverse. You can type out the outline or list and have it created in diagram form for you. Any text can be copied out of a different app and pasted into the app, as well. Once finished, your final product can be sent as an email to anyone. You can also save your diagram as a picture on the iPad and eventually download it to your computer.

One of the most obvious ways of using Idea Sketch is for its outlining capabilities. Students can type facts for their research project into it to keep everything straight. If they are making a slideshow presentation with other students, they can make an outline of it first and assign each other different parts, so everyone knows exactly what they are in charge of. They can also use it to plot out a story for a creative writing class. It can also be used as a simple list-making app. For younger students, Idea Sketch can be used to make a family tree. Even older students can make a more in-depth family tree to share with everyone.

Besides projects, Idea Sketch can be also used for day-to-day homework assignments. Before class, you can pre-make a diagram or flow chart with blank spots in it. This can then be emailed to your students email accounts. They can open it in their app and fill in the blanks as a warm up to the day's class or take it home and finish it there. It's a great way to test if they truly know their stuff.

Idea Sketch is a great way for both you and your student to keep all of your ideas in some sort of order. The app is free but can be upgraded for $3.99 to get more shapes, colors, and fonts, along with the ability to save your things as a PDF to save and print it from your computer. Students will love to be able to outline everything from the iPad, all while staying in the classroom.

Company: Nosleep Software
Size: 6.2 MB
Rating: 2.5 Stars
Grade Level: All

34
Khan Academy

Sometimes students just don't want to hear a teacher teach them something. They instead choose to tune you out and not pay attention at all. A good way of convincing them that you are, indeed, not making this stuff up is by showing them a video made by someone else. There are many websites where you can find videos, but sometimes the best things are free. By using the Khan Academy app, you can have all of their free videos from their website on your iPad.

Khan Academy provides 2,700 videos for classes of all ages and difficulty. This includes K-12 math, various sciences, and other topics like finance and history. You can easily download any of the videos within the app and take them with you to watch offline. With each video, you can also add subtitles. These subtitles can also be viewed in a list form at the bottom of each video to help you skip and scan to and through parts of each video. By creating an account and signing in, you can also keep track of your videos. It will remember how far you are in the video and show which ones you have already watched. In the future, the Khan Academy app will also feature quizzes you can give students after the video.

These videos are a great way for students to learn about nearly any topic. For example, if you want to learn about probability, there are 53 videos for you to choose from. Younger students can watch a video dealing with coin tossing. Older students can learn about the expected value of binomial distribution. The videos available can be used to teach the smarter kids in the class a concept ahead of time. They can also be used to review a concept before a unit test or something like the SAT. Everyone can learn these things at their own pace.

If you have each student create their own account, you can also assign watching the video as homework. The account will say if they really did or did not watch the video that night. This allows you to free up the class time it would require you to show it. You can even have the students fill out a worksheet as they watch the video for more practice. Since many students associate an iPad with fun and games, they will be more apt to watch the videos and learn from them.

By providing all of its videos for free, the Khan Academy app is the way to go for all classrooms. With the app also being free, students can easily learn any concept at any level. Some may even go and watch the video on their own accord without your assigning. They could easily find a topic that interests them and they want to learn more about. Students can easily watch a video during a break on the classroom iPad, if they wish. The facts they learn for the video can also provide information for a research project. Whatever the cause may be, everyone will benefit from the Khan Academy app.

Company: Khan Academy
Size: 1.8 MB
Rating: 4.5 Stars
Grade Level: All

35
Lino – Sticky and Photo Sharing for You

People can have an obsession with sticky notes. They may put them anywhere—in a notebook, on the fridge, in their bathroom, next to their bed—quite literally everywhere. These sticky notes may be to remind themselves of a due date, to remind them to ask or tell someone something, or as just a daily pick-me-up. Lino is the best way of using a virtual stick note without getting the mess and being able to share it with everyone.

The ultimate layout of the Lino app looks like a corkboard. Only, instead of using thumb tacks to hold up your note, you can stick your virtual sticky note onto the cork. You can add these sticky notes whenever you want, wherever you are. If you're offline, the note will show up when you become online again. These sticky notes can include memos, pictures and videos that you took, and even files. Everything can be organized by moving it around, changing its color, or adding an icon to its display. If the sticky is a reminder, you can even add a due date to it. This due date can then be synced to various other programs, like Google Calendar and Outlook. You can also get an email notification on the due day. Any and every memo can be deleted whenever you're done or finished with it. The board that you create can also be accessed online and shared with other students, teachers, or family for them to comment and post on.

Lino is the perfect way for you to keep in contact with your students, both in and out of the school day. With the ability to create different "canvases," you can have one for each class. You can post the due dates of various assignments and tests for everyone in the class to see. You can also use it to post notes of encouragements and reminders on other students' canvases. Lino is the perfect way to share pictures of school activities and field trips with students and their families, as well. It can also be used to advertise sports games and fundraisers.

Students can also use Lino for assignments. They can communicate with each other to see who's done what so far on a group project or offer suggestions to each other. Assignments can also be completed in the app. If you're in a classroom where students write a journal entry every day, you can now eliminate the use of paper. You can post the prompt on your canvas and have students put their reply on the same page. This allows you to grade them directly from your iPad. You can also assign and read their responses while you're gone or sick.

By using Lino, everyone will be able to communicate with each other. This free app is the perfect way to get important information around. Students can also use make each of their canvases uniquely their own by editing color, shape, and size of all the memos, photos, and videos. Now you'll truly never run out of sticky notes and places to put them.

Company: Inforteria Corporation
Size: 9.4 MB
Rating: 3 Stars
Grade Level: Middle – High School

36
Mobile Mouse Lite

Hate sitting behind your computer to change the slides of a slideshow? Don't feel comfortable asking a student to do it for you? Is your clicker out of batteries? All of these problems can be easily solved with the Mobile Mouse Lite app. It's quite literally what the title suggests—a mobile mouse. By using Mobile Mouse Lite, you can turn your classroom iPad into your very own portable keyboard and mouse.

Mobile Mouse Lite turns your iPad into the new portable keyboard—only this time much cheaper. The app features a touchpad that can be used in both vertical and landscape modes. It also includes a remote keyboard that you can easily hide and show. To hide or show it, all you have to do is shake the iPad. The keyboard will also work horizontally and vertically. You can even download the keyboard into different languages for language classrooms. For the mouse aspect of the app, it also has a scroll pad and a left and right clicker. Mobile Mouse Lite has no screen limitations. It will work with screens of any size and even multiple monitors. You can also add password protection to prevent students from using the app if there is only one iPad in your room. By upgrading the app for $1.99, you can get even more features. These include an application switcher, a file browser, a numeric keyboard, the ability to wake a sleeping computer, and even more. Before using it on any computer, all you need to do is download the software for free from their website. This will set you up with a username to assign your app to so it knows exactly what computer it is dealing with.

92 Amazing Apps for Teachers

Teachers can easily make use of this app in any classroom setting. If your room features a projector, you can teach from your iPad without having to sit behind the computer. You can use it anywhere from simply changing slides on a presentation, to using it for things like changing between different programs or website links. If a spur-of-the-moment question comes up from a student, you can also look up the question directly from the front of the classroom. Many students will feel more engaged in the lesson if you spend the whole thing in front of them, instead of behind your computer.

Students can also benefit from the Mobile Mouse Lite App. If they want to explain or show the class something, they can easily be handed the iPad in a keyboard/mouse form to explain everything on the screen directly from their seat. This can also be used to help solve problems. You can make an interactive document that students have to move something around on and have them solve it directly from their seats by looking at the projector screen.

By downloading the Mobile Mouse Lite app for your classroom's iPad, you will be doing everyone a favor. No longer will you be isolated behind your computer during the days lecture or lesson. Instead, you will be in front of the entire class. Students will also enjoy the much more interactive classroom environment.

Company: RPA Tech Inc
Size: 7.0 MB
Rating: 4 Stars
Grade Level: All

37
Molecules

Everyone will end up learning about molecules at some point in their school career. Students may even learn about them in different grades and various classes at different levels. Even though most people can be set in their ways on what type of diagram they like to use to explain their structure, the Molecules app offers yet another option.

Molecules displays a large variety of various three-dimensional figures. The app allows you to easily manipulate the molecule. You can rotate the entire thing or zoom in and out of various parts of it. While zoomed in, you can also pan around the screen to other various parts. The whole layout is very natural. New molecules can be downloaded from a set of websites. These can be saved to your device and viewed at any time. Custom-made molecules can be downloaded from an online link or from the app store. You can also change the way each molecule is viewed. One way is by showing each atom as a round ball with spaces in between each one. The other way is, again, by showing each atom as a ball and then having every one connected by a stick. In the description of each molecule, you can also see how many atoms are in it.

The Molecules app is a great way for students to learn and play around with different molecules of various sizes. Students can easily have fun with the included molecules and the ones you choose to download. Some of these pre-loaded molecules include DNA, caffeine, and insulin. You can have students identify the parts of the molecules by labeling their atoms, or trying to figure out what molecule it is they are looking at. By using the screen-shot feature of the iPad, you can also take a picture of a molecule. This can then be emailed for the students to view at home.

If your classroom only has one iPad, students will have fun taking turns manipulating the molecule. If everyone has an iPad, it'll be a great way to spend a class period. Students of all ages will look forward to learning from the app. As a free app, Molecules can be insanely addictive, and you may find even yourself being impressed by the complexity of some atoms.

Company: Brad Larson
Size: 1.0 MB
Rating: 4.5 Stars
Grade Level: Middle – High School

38
Musée du Louvre

Even if you know next to nothing about art, you've at least hopefully heard of the Louvre. If you haven't heard of the museum, then you've no doubt heard of the things that are available to view within it—things like the Mona Lisa, the Last Supper, famous Greek sculptures, and paintings by Raphael. Though these things are important to our world's culture, chances are slim that you will ever be able to take a class field trip to this iconic place. However, by downloading the Musée du Louvre app, you can easily bring this museum to the classroom.

The Musée du Louvre app is a great way to show classic art in the classroom. The app features over 100 different pieces of artwork that are on display at the Louvre in France. The app also has over 500 built-in pictures of these pieces of art. You can easily zoom in on these pictures to view them in even greater detail. It also includes videos describing each piece of artwork and an introductory video giving a basic tour of the actual Louvre museum. If your class is fortunate to visit this place, the app will also provide a list of upcoming events taking place there. You can also view the Visitor Center to help plan your trip to the museum.

Whether you're a history or art classroom, your students will love paging through this app. It's the perfect way to learn to appreciate the artwork of our past. The app can be used in many different ways. Students can use it for amusement by just looking through the many different things that available to see there. It may even inspire them to go travel there someday.

However, the Musée du Louvre app can be used for so much more than just a way to pass the time. It can easily allow students to interpret art. You can have them view any piece and then have them write about it. How they choose to write about them can be up to the student or predetermined. Things they could write about include their interpretation of it, its history, the techniques used to make it, or what it means to them. The chosen art piece can be any random one or something that fits in with the time period you are currently learning about in class.

This free app is a great way for students to learn to appreciate artwork. Many middle-aged to older students will have lots of fun seeing what people were able to make hundreds of years ago. If the classroom only has one iPad, they can all take turns. If everyone has their own, they can all look at these truly one-of-a-kind works of art on their own. Most will be amazed to figure out that is only a small portion of what can be viewed at the famous Louvre museum.

Company: MUSEE DU LOUVRE
Size: 813 MB
Rating: 4 Stars
Grade Level: Middle – High School

39
neu.Annotate

Perfect for group projects, presentations, and research in and out of the classroom, the neu.Annotate app gives teachers an amazing amount of flexibility when using it during their courses. With this app, you can read and annotate PDF documents, using great features like drawings, text notes, highlighting text, stamps, and photos. The best thing about it is that the newly annotated documents are then still compatible with both Adobe Acrobat and Apple Preview programs.

The neu.Annotate app has become a favorite of teachers because it supports documents in so many different types of programs. In essence, it can open PDF files from any application supporting the "Open with" menu command, including Safari, Mail, MobileMe, Dropbox, and more. The files may also be imported through iTunes file sharing.

Once teachers or students have annotated PDF documents, they can then be shared through a variety of settings, including email, iTunes, and Dropbox. Plus, the individual pages may also be shared in JPG or PNG formats, if needed.

For educators looking for new ways to allow their students to create and analyze, neu.Annotate is a great option. It makes adding notes and drawings to PDFs easy, and teachers can even use them for exams because students can fill information into them. This makes test taking much more interactive and allows educators more flexibility in assigning projects to students or groups of students.

Another reason this app is increasing in popularity in the education world is because it encourages collaboration between teachers and students. Students working on group projects at home can share their annotated PDFs via email or a system like Dropbox, giving them the power to work together even if they're not in the same physical location. Teachers, for their part, can receive assignments via email for added convenience.

The neu.Annotate app has a great deal of potential for educators to enhance their curriculum, to the obvious benefit of their students.

Company: neu.Pen LLC
Size: 20.7 MB
Rating: 4+
Appropriate for Grade Levels: 6-12

40
neu.Notes

Take interactive notes like never before with the highly versatile, incredibly functional neu.Notes app for your iPad. This application allows you to take notes in a variety of different ways, save them, and study them later for a greater learning experience. What really sets it apart from other note-taking apps is its ability to allow you to choose from a number of actions, properties, and tools to best customize your note-taking experience. Save your apps right on your iPad or export them as PNG files to review them on other mediums.

neu.Notes is your equivalent to a digital sketchpad. The app features a number of different pen and brush tools to give your notes the diversity that you've always wanted. Use different colors to annotate your drawings or simply add dimension to pictures for an enhanced note-taking experience.

Once you've sketched out an assortment of notes, drawings, and reminders, neu.Notes gives you the unique ability to reorganize and reorder them visually. Now you can craft notes that have a common theme and arrange them in a linear fashion for coherent learning and review. Tag different notes for added organization and search different tags to recall older notes whenever you need to review them.

Using neu.Notes is easy for all ages. Because the app is self-explanatory and has virtually no learning curve, anyone can pick it up, sketch a note and file it for later. One of the fastest note-taking apps on the rise today, neu.Notes is gaining a huge following thanks to its ability to teach students about the importance of good note-taking and organization. Teachers can encourage good note-taking with the app's easy to use drawing interface and educate their students on how to take a series of notes on a single subject.

Teachers who are looking for the easiest way to enhance their student's note-taking ability can turn to neu.Notes and expect nothing short of phenomenal results.

Company: neu.Pen LLC
Size: 9.2 MB
Rating: 4.5
Appropriate for Grade Levels: 4-12

41
Overdrive

When it comes to providing extra resources for classroom learning, Overdrive tops the list with an almost infinite number of learning supplements. This virtual library gives students and teachers alike the ability to browse from a vast selection of digital books, both fiction and non-fiction, from your local library and check them out digitally on your iDevice. Requiring only a valid library card and a free Adobe Online ID, you'll have thousands of titles in the palm of your hand—free of charge and ready to read in just minutes.

Overdrive is the newest innovation in eBook technology and gives classrooms a free solution to supplementing learning. Great for book reports and background reading, this app allows you access to books without having to pay checkout fees or even leave the classroom. Now, teachers and students can collaborate over reading materials together, instead of separately between the classroom and home.

Both eBooks and audio books are available through Overdrive, enhancing your ability to teach or learn. Complete with easily segmented sections and resizable text for optimal reading, eBooks rented through Overdrive are designed to fit anyone's needs. This intelligently designed app even features learning tools that aren't available through traditional means of research—like a built-in dictionary feature that helps students define key words and phrases right in the app.

What's more, you'll be able to keep Overdrive eBooks and audio books for up to 21 days, depending on your library source. When it's time to return the book, you won't have to deal with traditional library late fees or other charges: the book simply returns itself digitally in case you forgot.

Make the most out of book reports, extracurricular reading assignments, or course supplemental reading with Overdrive. This app makes renting, reading, and listening to books easy enough for any age group and can greatly enhance a student's learning experience, as well as a teacher's ability to expand upon a topic through the joys of reading.

Company: Overdrive, Inc.
Size: 9.2 MB
Rating: 4.5
Appropriate for Grade Levels: 4-12

42
Paper 53

Turning your iPad into a blank canvas has never been easier than it is with Paper 53. Capture ideas in sketches, outlines, text, and watercolor to create beautiful, digital works of art. This exceptionally designed app can unleash the creativity of anyone and makes it easy to communicate ideas through art. Plus, with a vast array of touch technology features, such as two finger swiping and innovative scrolling, you'll never be at a loss for great functionality.

Paper 53 utilizes an enormous library of different brush strokes, colors, and swatches to turn any situation into an artistic experience. Great for helping students communicate their ideas through pictures and drawings, this app is geared toward unleashing your inner artist and promoting cognitive development through expression.

The simplicity of Paper 53 lends itself to any user group. For those who struggle with art and expression, this app provides a no-nonsense approach to creativity by offering no distractions—just a blank slate for ideas to flow. For users of this app who are artistically inclined, there are plenty of options to help customize the drawing experience, making it unique to everyone's needs.

With Paper 53, art class instantly becomes more alluring and a whole lot easier to clean up. Students who exhibit no interest in art can captivate themselves with a digital complement to a pen and paper, while those who take pride in their artistic interests can immerse themselves in a world where any type of art is possible. Because Paper 53 is completely digital and fluidly accurate, the times of spending precious resources on art supplies are a thing of the past. Now, instead of cutting arts from our schools, we can bring the curriculum into the future—a future that is cost effective and still wildly imaginative.

With so many versatile tools built into a single, sophisticated app, Paper 53 redefines what it means to bring art into the lives of developing students.

Company: Fifty Three Inc.
Size: 27.52 MB
Rating: 4.5
Appropriate for Grade Levels: 5-12

43
PaperPort

Just when you thought that taking notes couldn't get any easier, an app like PaperPort comes along and changes your perception on what it means to dictate your own learning experience. Quite literally, this voice-to-text app gives students the ability to take their own notes by simply talking to their iPhone or iPad. Likewise, teachers can easily record slides, handouts, lectures, and other transcripts with ease, bridging the gap between thought and text.

PaperPort serves the dual focus of providing an easy way to transcribe notes, as well as catering to those whose typing skills aren't quite up to pace with their listening and speaking abilities. Superbly accurate and unsurpassed when it comes to speed, this app bring the note-taking process to a whole new level.

Organize your virtual notes right in the app, no matter if it's text, pictures, drawings or audio clips, and easily share them across multiple platforms. Connect via email, Google Docs, Dropbox, and a number of other digital sharing mediums, or simply print your notes at your convenience to study or share them. PaperPort makes streaming notes across all of your iDevices easy and seamless.

For students who like to multitask and make maximum use of their time or for those who simply prefer speaking over writing, PaperPort can be fine tuned to meet your expectations. Plus, the interfacing of this app even allows you to customize the look and feel of your notes based on the content. Choose a traditional ruled paper look for basic school notes or dabble with a graphing page for math and science-based learning. You can even select images and previously typed pages to annotate and mark up for optimal studying.

For teachers looking to motivate their students with interactive notes or simply for making the learning process more diverse, there's PaperPort—a streamlined way to make your notes completely unique and thoroughly inviting.

Company: Nuance Communications
Size: 4.5 MB
Rating: 4.5
Appropriate for Grade Levels: 3-12

44
pClock

Students often live their lives by the hands on a clock, as class schedules, lunch periods, starts, and stops are all dictated by time. Why not make the perpetual clock a bit more interesting with pClock? This interactive, customizable clock will encourage more students to keep track of time and hone time management skills for future applications. Pick your own pictures, personal photos, and other images, set them to this handy clock app and watch as the hands of time are suddenly more interesting than the plain old black and white that we're used to.

No matter what photos you select, they'll be displayed conveniently as the background of a working analog clock. To correspond with the designated pictures, the clock facing can also be customized with different colors that make it stand out every time. Relocate the clock anywhere on the page with a simple dragging motion and change the size to best fit your needs—all within pClock.

Great for timed testing and time management lessons, pClock is a lightweight app that will always give your student the exact time. Use this faultless clock to set start times, stop times, and other designations that will help engrain the importance of self-paced tasks within a developing student.

pClock's exceptional ability to function fluidly and flawlessly means you'll never have to worry about lagging animation and faulted times. You can also save your clock layouts for future use, meaning you'll never have to rebuild your interface when you open the app.

Keep an eye on the time in style with pClock. Upload pictures directly from your camera app or pull images from pClock's extensive library of images to create a clock that's both personable to your tastes and will give you an accurate idea of how to manage your time.

Company: Wan-gon Park
Size: 3.2 MB
Rating: 4.5
Appropriate for Grade Levels: 4-12

45
PhysicalSci

Science teachers who are looking for a fun and interactive way to educate their students on matter, energy, and change now have a treasure trove of resources in the palm of their hand with the PhysicalSci app for iPhone and iPad. This highly valuable tool for teaching core physical science theories offers an abundant number of concepts, interactive learning modules, and experiments to further a student's understanding of relevant topics.

PhysicalSci sports well-organized units of study that focus on concepts learned in the classroom. Educators can rely on this app to help their students experience and learn from real-world examples in a virtual setting that's both captivating and easy to use. Plus, in-app quizzes and detailed flashcards make it effortless to review course material with this additional information.

Complete with an extensive glossary of terms and theories, the PhysicalSci app easily intertwines with in-class material that is taught by the teacher. Thanks to the high-quality video examples, expertly crafted charts and interactive interface of this app, many teachers have even begun to use PhysicalSci as a direct teaching method in class. Another great feature of PhysicalSci is the animations and simulations. This feature allows students to see the scientific words described through moving pictures. Having the definitions show in both words and picture helps to teach all students with all types of learning styles.

Geared toward middle school and high school students, this app is easily adopted by anyone looking to teach or learn concepts of physical science. Right from the get-go of opening this app, you'll have the tools at your disposal to instantly refine topics taught in the classroom. It works exceptionally well as a study guide or course supplement and can save a teacher time by offering further explanations of topics that aren't always addressed in textbooks or prepared lectures.

PhysicalSci is a great way into integrate multiple methods of teaching in the classroom, through the animations, videos, and simulations. This app is a great way to integrate technology into the classroom, as well introduce students to this format of independent study, which they are likely to use in the future. PhysicalSci is one of the best free science studying apps available to teachers and students and is a great asset to integrate into both classroom and individual instruction.

Bring the wonders of science to your iDevice with the PhysicalSci app. The gorgeously prepared design and seamless navigation of this app will enrich the learning experience for any physical science student.

Company: CPO Science
Size: 11.8 MB
Rating: 5
Appropriate for Grade Levels: 6-12

46
Polldaddy

Feedback and polling can generate some of the most useful data for an educator, as well as provide a two-way communication medium for students. Polldaddy aims to close the communication gap between teachers and students by offering a great tool that addresses both questions and answers in the classroom. This artfully designed app makes it easy to pose questions and elicit responses from an entire group of people.

The PollDaddy app works with www.PollDaddy.com accounts in writing and creating your own surveys. PollDaddy.com allows you to choose a plan and price that works for you, and then they assist you in creating surveys on the topic of your choice. The PollDaddy app allows you to take the surveys you create into the classroom or anywhere else you choose.

Consider this: a test-like scenario in which an entire class can participate with the simple tap of a button, contributing their answers anonymously, yet at the same time. This technology has existed for years, but hasn't been refined like it is within the Polldaddy app. This app gives you the opportunity to conduct a lecture and gain feedback from everyone involved without taking the time to prepare a test packet or arrange a testing site.

The way Polldaddy works is simple. All you need to do is program a number of questions and responses into the app, either about a lecture or about a topic. When the question is asked, students can refer to their iPhone or iPad to select their answer and contribute their response to the ongoing poll data. As an educator, all you'll need to do is access the questionnaire and check the responses to easily and accurate gauge a consensus.

How do you retrieve the precious data that you're looking for if everyone has their own smartphone or tablet? Easy. Polldaddy features a great tool that lets each student upload his or her completed survey to your online Polldaddy account. Once the surveys are uploaded, data is tabulated and available for analysis—all in one single place. It makes getting a straight answer no trouble at all.

Open the lines of communication in your classroom and shed some light on what your students have to say with the Polldaddy app. Not only will you have a direct line of feedback and to your lectures and topics, you'll have the attention of your class, as well.

Company: Automattic, Inc.
Size: 4.2 MB
Rating: 2.5
Appropriate for Grade Levels: 6-12

47
Pop Math Lite

Math can be a hard subject for most students to master, especially at a young age. Giving children the fundamentals of math in an easy-to-use, engaging medium is easier than ever, thanks to Pop Math Lite. This quick to learn, easy-to-master game masks the sometimes less than desirable task of learning basic math with a fun, game-like atmosphere. Your students won't even realize that they're learning the building blocks of math—they'll be having too much fun mastering number sequences in this engaging environment.

Pop Math Lite goes above and beyond traditional number games to provide your students with an amicable way of learning different math equations. By popping bubbles that contain basic equations and single numbers, students will learn the value of basic math. Progression through the game gives way to more complicated bubbles in an effort to encourage continued participation in this unique setting.

To help your students learn from their mistakes, Pop Math Lite also features a reporting system that will identify the number of incorrect math problems that a student picked, scoring them based on their accuracy. A score clock also encourages players to beat their fastest times, allowing for improvement in quickness and response time.

Even children who can't be bothered by math won't be able to put this highly addictive game down. By delivering math in a way that inspires children to think outside the box, Pop Math Lite delivers results on a level that repetition and flashcards just can't match. In an age where traditional mediums might not spark a child's curiosity, this innovative response to basic math surely will.

Addition, subtraction, multiplication, and division can all be given the proper basis for future math development, thanks to Pop Math Lite. Create the perfect environment to foster learning mathematics with this exceptional app.

Company: AppBlit LLC
Size: 0.5 MB
Rating: 3.5
Appropriate for Grade Levels: 2-6

48
Popplet Lite

Sometimes all it takes for great development in a student is a visual representation of what they're thinking. Popplet Lite makes mind mapping and sequencing easy to do and beautiful to look at, all in a digital medium that can support a student's every thought. This great iPad app can help clear the mind, illustrate an idea, and have it all come together right before your eyes.

Popplet Lite starts with an idea—something on a child's mind that he or she can't seem to elaborate on or need help visualizing. This idea is put into the app and given a visual representation, whether it's a picture, text, or something else. From there, it becomes effortless to draw new ideas and expand upon theories, connecting them visually to the original idea. Before you know it, your student will have a fully formed idea right in front of them, ready to be put into action.

Create multiple webs on a single page to intertwine ideas, or stick with a single conceptualization and expand on different angles—either choice is yours with Popplet Lite. And students aren't the only benefactors of this highly versatile app; educators can plot their own ideas, as well. Craft a lesson plan, freely associate ideas, and create projects in an easy-to-communicate environment that gives you free reign over your ideas.

What truly makes Popplet great is its ability to incorporate all of your ideas through a variety of different tools. Use pictures to represent ideas or text to jot notes. You can even move snippets of information in your sequenced web to give your idea the life it needs to properly take shape.

Whether you're looking to finesse ideas from a convoluted mind or just want to arrange your thoughts in a visual manner, Popplet Lite is an invaluable tool for any educator. With all of the functionality and ease of use, even your students can use this handy app to map out a thought.

Company: Notion, Inc.
Size: 19.0 MB
Rating: 4.0
Appropriate for Grade Levels: 4-8

49
Presentation Clock

Presentation Clock is a simple, yet incredibly useful, app. Presentation Clock serves as a timekeeper with an endless list of uses. This app clearly displays large, easy-to-read numbers that count down from the time you choose. For just $.99, this app will eliminate the need for large time cards or loud and obnoxious beeping timers and provide you with a simple and efficient timing method.

Unique to this app, the color of the clock changes as the time counts down. The numbers will start as green. Presentation Clock then allows you to choose when the color turns to yellow and eventually when you would like the background to change to red, signaling that the presenter is nearing the end of the allotted time.

This app is perfect for classes with one classroom iPad, as it displays the numbers big enough to be seen from quite a distance, making it perfect for classroom presentations and speeches. When a class has several iPads, this app is great for practicing in groups or in pairs.

This app works wonderfully for all age levels. At a high school and middle school level, this app is perfect for speeches and presentations, as well as for timed test taking. At the elementary school level, this app can be used for any sort of timed activity, whether it is multiplication facts or races to see who can say the alphabet in less than 20 seconds. Presentation Clock does it all.

When the timer has ended, Presentation Clock also has the added convenience of counting back up after the timer runs out to help monitor any excess over the time limit. Presentation Clock allows you to choose a sounded, vibrating, or silent alarm when the time has run out.

Presentation Clock also allows you to save set timers for the future, as well as pause timers that have already been started. Presentation Clock sets timers anywhere for one second to 99 minutes, and anywhere in between. This app also works well when blown-up onto a larger screen for full-class viewing.

Using timing in the classroom is a great way to get students involved in an activity. Younger kids respond well to being timed, because it promotes a competitive aspect that encourages kids to do their best. Elementary students enjoy doing things with a clock, no matter how simple. Anything from times tables to listing the fifty states in less than two minutes adds extra excitement to classes. For middle and high school students, working with a timer in class helps them build valuable time management skills that will benefit them in future test taking and presenting opportunities.

As a simple alternative to the classic loud buzzer clocks and time cards, Presentation Clock is a great way to save time and improve the level of technology in you classroom. This-easy-to-use app is sure to make timing in your classroom as simple as possible.

Company: Shawn Welch
Size: Size: 5.8 MB
Rating: 4.0
Appropriate for Grade Levels: All

50
Prezi Viewer

Using a virtual canvas to paint pictures, share ideas, and explore new methods of teaching can be one of the greatest tools in a teacher's arsenal. Prezi Viewer gives you the ability to do this and more, thanks to its cloud computing abilities and convenient interfacing options. Your presentations will never be the same thanks to the astounding features available in this app and the fluidity in which they can be edited.

What really sets Prezi Viewer apart from other slideshow and presentation apps is its zooming aspect and multi-touch gestures. Not only can you get up close and personal with a slideshow, but you can also examine it from every possible angle to get the most out of your teaching materials. Revise, retouch, and interject new ideas into a presentation on the fly with this great app.

Prezi Viewer can be your prime solution to a common classroom scenario. Nowadays, a teacher's staple in the classroom is often a slideshow or visual presentation. Because children are visual learners and benefit from aesthetic examples, it's in your best interests to create a lecture that's both visual and informative. With Prezi Viewer, you won't have to worry about your creations breaching the barrier into mundane repetition from day to day. Instead, you'll be able to shed new light on topics like never before, thanks to all of the neat features included in this app.

Bridge your lectures with an artfully crafted Prezi Viewer presentation and watch as the knowledge that you're communicating takes hold in a classroom like never before. By using this highly advanced technology to reinforce core ideas and encourage interactive learning, you'll open the door to new questions, refined ideas, and free association in the minds of your students.

If your presentations could use a bit more style, a few last minute tweaks, or a whole new spin to keep them interesting, don't hesitate to invest your time in Prezi Viewer.

Company: Prezi, Inc.
Size: 12.7 MB
Rating: 4.5
Appropriate for Grade Levels: 6-12

51
Price Grabber

Originally created to be a source of smart shopping and price comparisons, Price Grabber is fast becoming an educational tool, as well. This app gives you all of the tools that you need to teach your students about real-world commerce and instill ideas about economic functions that they can take with them throughout life.

Because Price Grabber features goods from all industries and walks of life, it's a great tool for teaching your students the interconnectivity of macroeconomics. Which industries affect other industries? Are there industries that depend on one another to survive, grow, and flourish? These are the types of questions that you're able to pose and address, thanks to this app's excellent layout.

Another great topic to discuss with Price Grabber is the fluctuation and importance of prices in a free market economy. Thanks to its data feeds that feature price changes, you and your students will be able to explore the ever-changing concepts of inflation, recession, and actual value when it comes to real life examples in this app.

The biggest lesson of all that you'll gain with Price Grabber is the idea of competition. Because it's meant to act as a price comparison app, Price Grabber will display different vendors and their prices so you can directly see how companies compete with one another and what types of tactics they use while doing so.

Because Price Grabber is a real-time app, you also have the added advantage of viewing market trends as they happen. When prices drop or top competitors change, you'll be there to see it and pose the question to your students, "What happened, and why did it happen?" Use the price tracking software to keep tabs on different companies and explore their solution to competition in a free market, using this app as a practical example for your lesson plan.

Explore all of the interesting aspects of business, economics, and competition with the Price Grabber app. By using this app to help your students analyze real world examples and timeless economic trends, you'll be thinking outside of the normal lesson plan to deliver a unique teaching experience.

Company: PriceGrabber.com, Inc.
Size: 5.3 MB
Rating: 2.5
Appropriate for Grade Levels: 8-12

52
Puffin

Puffin is a great alternative web browser for your iPhone or iPad and lends itself to the classroom in a number of ways where stock web browsing apps fall short. It's an extremely lightweight, super-fast product that delivers instantaneous search results and web browsing without the annoying wait times. Puffin will immediately reduce your load times and turn your classroom into an on-demand content searching machine.

What separates Puffin from other web browsing apps is its ability to handle multiple unique tasks at once in a flexible environment. You can simultaneously search pictures, video, and text across different windows to bring an online learning experience into a single frame of reference. What's more, Puffin handles content that other mobile browsing apps don't—like flash video.

With so many unique and different ways to search the web, your teaching possibilities are limitless. Task the Puffin browser with finding and saving your lecture information so you can bring up an entire array of information with the tap of an app. The best part is Puffin is advertisement free, leaving you with no distractions when displaying your online materials.

If you're teaching a subject and need supporting materials to really bring the point home, Puffin can instantly lend its support to your topic. It loads complete web pages in seconds and renders them with beautiful precision and detail, meaning you'll never be at a loss for crystal clear examples. And, if you're the kind of teacher who likes to save great examples for future lectures and classroom discussions, Puffin supports an excellent bookmarking system that will always save your content in a reliable way.

Open your world to endless possibilities with the quick and easy controls of Puffin. This highly advanced web browser will lend itself to your classroom again and again as you seek to provide the best virtual learning possible.

Company: CloudMosa, Inc.
Size: 7.3 MB
Rating: 3.5
Appropriate for Grade Levels: 11-12

53
Puppet Pals HD

Storytelling is a great way to encourage participation, build a foundation for public speaking, and instill confidence in a child. With Puppet Pals HD, your students will have the ability to instantly create and share their very own stories, thanks to the wonderful tools at their disposal in this easy-to-use app. With a multitude of different features and interactive involvement, Puppet Pals HD will put a whole new spin on story time and sharing.

Great for a younger audience of developing kids, Puppet Pals HD provides the basic tools for telling a story in a way that's engaging and interactive: sparking interest in young minds and encouraging group participation when kids are most prone to shy away. This app is great for classroom sharing and works exceptionally well when compiling group projects into a full-length story-like presentation.

The app works by supplying a number of custom characters, as well as allowing you to import photos of students so they can be created as characters in a virtual story. By adding puppets, background scenes, photos, and more, you can easily craft a story that can also be narrated. After you narrate a story, just interject the audio in the animated story and watch as the movies comes to life right before your eyes.

Give each student a part in the movie or encourage him or her to write their own dialogue to bring an entire class together in a never before seen way. When it's complete, hook up your iPhone or iPad to a computer or projector to play your creation and let everyone involved enjoy the great work they contributed.

Puppet Pals HD could be exactly what you're looking for to help build a firm foundation for future social skills in students. Public speaking, group interaction, and task management are all key concepts that can be learned from a simple, enjoyable app like Puppet Pals HD.

Company: Polished Play LLC
Size: 22.7 MB
Rating: 4.0
Appropriate for Grade Levels: 1-5

54
QuickVoice

Looking for a quick way to take notes, leave yourself a reminder, or record a lecture digitally? QuickVoice is an aptly named app that will enable you to do all of that and more, thanks to its stellar recording software. The apps works much like a small recording studio, allowing you to record a snippet of sound and replay it again later at your convenience.

Whether you're talking for a few seconds or a few hours, you can trust that this app will get it all recorded and ready to replay with numerous features. Pause, rewind, fast forward, or select a specific chunk of audio to listen to—all with simple swiping technology and a few taps.

If you're hosting an online classroom or virtual learning community, this app has infinite value in its ability to export audio tracks to different website or a PC. Label your audio snippets for increased organization and view details on the go, such as length, date recorded, and total file size.

With QuickVoice, you can record complementary audio for any lecture or presentation you're giving, as an audio supplement for a visual learning experience. Record the perfect audio lecture in sync with presentations as you walk through step-by-step, then include the audio later for a cohesive project. It's that simple.

If you're good at multitasking, then this app is clearly for you. Now you can record perfect notes and abundant amounts of information without taking the time to write it all down. You can even use other apps while QuickVoice works in the background to reach your peak performance levels.

The next time you need to take quick notes or record audio for something, don't hesitate to choose a teacher's best friend: QuickVoice. You'll have crisp, clean audio tracks at your disposal, ready to be used when you need them.

Company: nFinity Inc.
Size: 0.5 MB
Rating: 3.5
Appropriate for Grade Levels: 4-12

55
Redlaser

QR codes are popping up all over the place and are serving new purposes each and every day. In the classroom, QR codes are becoming an easy way to share information, link topics together, and view news, but without a proper QR code reader, some people might never have access to this information. Redlaser is the perfect complement to your iPhone and can instantly decipher any QR code, giving you access to all of its information and resources.

With Redlaser, a whole new spectrum of information is opened up and at your disposal. Consider what it would mean to have a student hand in a physical paper with their works cited information in the form of a scan-able QR code—no need to request a digital copy to click on links or, worse yet, type in a convoluted web address. What's more, you'll be able to hand back a physical copy of their paper with comments corrections and suggestions, instead of giving feedback digitally.

However, Redlaser doesn't just limit your scanning abilities to QR codes. If you're running low on school supplies and need to purchase more, you're going to want to get the best information about what you're buying. Scan the barcode on your product and watch as Redlaser instantly retrieves your results, giving you plenty of options on where to buy it, as well.

With barcode and QR code technology sweeping the world, you're going to want a reliable, instantaneous way to decrypt these useful symbols. Redlaser is that tool and never fails to bring you up to speed on the information stored in a barcode. Whether it's a link to a website, access to a hidden message, or promotion by a social media network, you'll be able to view it with Redlaser.

Company: Occipital, LLC
Size: 3.7 MB
Rating: 3.0
Appropriate for Grade Levels: 7-12

56
SAS Flash Cards

Create. Understand. Remember. Those are the goals when it comes to learning information with the help of the SAS Flash Cards app. This app takes traditional flashcards to the next level and gives you the ability to create an interactive study medium right on your iPhone or iPad. Program different questions, subjects, and answers into this app and quiz yourself anywhere at any time.

Teachers can create and upload different subject decks to the Internet, which in turn can be downloaded by students to improve study habits and increase understanding of core subject matter values. This invaluable tool can likewise be used from a student perspective, to program subjects that need extra attention right into their smartphone or tablet. From there, the possibilities are limitless for crafting great study habits and organizational skills.

Whether you're working with plain text, pictures, or other visual representations, SAS Flash Cards is an excellent way to organize the information in a question/answer-based format. Choose from multiple choice, direct answer, or best answer formats to increase coherency about a subject and help students make good decisions in their answers.

SAS Flash Cards also supports features that tower over other flashcard apps—like the ability to take notes about your different cards. If your student is flipping through cards and consistently gets stuck on a question, you also have the ability to mark that card for later review. Or, for a student on the go, the auto play function in SAS Flash Cards can recite audio facts without the need for visual supplements.

Set up both practice and quiz modes to simulate real-time studying habits and timed quizzes, ensuring that your student is best prepared for anything in a test-like environment. With so many different options and a sleek, easy-to-learn interface and a multitude of possibilities, SAS Flash Cards is a must-have for any student who takes studying seriously.

Company: SAS Institute, Inc.
Size: 8.8 MB
Rating: 4.5
Appropriate for Grade Levels: 4-12

57
Scan

Just when you thought digital sharing couldn't get any faster, QR codes hit the scene and created the simplest way to get a point across. Just by scanning one of these special barcodes, you'll be able to open the door to a number of interactive learning experiences that expound upon traditional learning in a way that was never before thought possible. However, unless you have the Scan app, you're going to have a hard time unlocking the door to brand-new educational experiences.

This app allows you to simply point your iPhone's camera at a QR code and have it automatically scan the data encrypted. Whatever is coded within the QR code will be interpreted by Scan, and you'll be given numerous possibilities when it comes to executing the data. Open a webpage, watch a video, or follow a new social media network—the choice is yours, depending on the QR code.

In the classroom, you'll find special uses for Scan that you'd never think to use otherwise. Assign preprogrammed QR codes to students and scan them in as a form of attendance or use it to assign different groups to different projects. You can even use Scan to open individual grades for a student when it comes time to discuss them.

Scan provides a number of features that other barcode readers just don't have, making it a great addition to your classroom experience. The app features a history tab that allows you to label and recall past QR scans in an effort to save time. It also syncs across multiple devices, meaning you'll always have a record of previous scans at your disposal.

If you're really excited about the possibilities of QR code technology and want to use Scan to its fullest potential, consider basing an entire lecture on QR codes. Assemble all of your media in the form of QR codes and create an interactive presentation by scanning each code with Scan to illustrate a new idea.

Company: QR Code City, LLC
Size: 6.2 MB
Rating: 4.5
Appropriate for Grade Levels: 7-12

58
Science360

Exploring the wide world of scientific advancements has never been easier than it is with the Science360 app. Thanks to this beautifully designed, highly functional iPad and iPhone app, you'll be able to keep your students engaged with daily breakthroughs in all areas of the scientific community. It displays live news feeds and breaking stories in all areas of physical and theoretical science, in a way that's easily understood by anyone reading.

Science360 was designed by the National Science Foundation as a way to educate students of all ages on the changing world around them. From the moment you open this app, you'll be captivated by the endless streams of scientific research, studies, and breakthroughs that grab your attention.

Experience news stories, photos, and amazing videos all from within this real-time app, and teach your students about the wonders of science with the most up-to-date information available. And, because Science360 brings everything together in a single place, you won't have to search endlessly for facts and snippets of information to really expand upon a topic.

If you're looking to teach a particular topic, use the excellent search function within this app to pinpoint exactly what you're seeking. Everything from Archaebacteria to Zoology is at your fingertips and can lead you in the right direction when it comes to easily teaching students about these abundant topics.

If you happen to stumble upon a great news story, cool idea, or thought-provoking segment while browsing Science360, don't fret at the thought of forgetting it—simply save it to the app for a later date. The app will keep a record of saves for interesting topics that you designate and allow you to effortlessly access and share them at any time.

Bring the wonderful world of science into your classroom with the superb Science360 app and always be sure that you're teaching the newest, most accurate scientific findings.

Company: National Science Foundation
Size: 11.0 MB
Rating: 3.5
Appropriate for Grade Levels: 3-12

59
Scratchwork

Many math-based apps just don't cut it when it comes to upper-level math courses at school. Likewise, many note-taking apps don't cater to math courses and can leave your students frustrated and with poor notes. Solve both of these problems with Scratchwork and watch as notes become more coherent, especially when it comes to more complicated math courses.

Scratchwork's claim to fame is an interface that allows you to open a web browser right alongside a notepad. This dual screen combination allows students to view material from the Internet and take notes at the same time, eliminating the need to switch back and forth between apps or spend time between a notebook and their iPad or iPhone.

The built-in, specially designed math calculator that's featured in Scratchwork is one of a kind and can handle some very complicated math equations. It also gives students the versatility to plot functions—something that other apps just don't offer when it comes to calculations. Insert graphs, images, and sketches to complement your notes and take them to the next level.

When it's time to export notes, students can easily send Scratchwork markups to their email accounts in the form of an easy-to-read PDF file. From there, it's only a few simple steps to print hard copies of previously drawn notes. Or, if your classroom features an Apple Airport wireless system, you can have students print directly from an iPhone or iPad.

Note-taking is one of the most important skills a student can learn. Promote great note-taking in your classroom with Scratchwork and watch as the skills of your students begin to take shape and grow. This app promotes interactivity in the note-taking process, allowing students to incorporate multimedia sources to further their learning experience.

Company: Daniel Soffer
Size: 9.5 MB
Rating: 3.0
Appropriate for Grade Levels: 7-12

60
Screenchomp

Want to explain a concept in simplest terms? Why not make a little video tutorial about it? Screenchomp gives you the power to record your every move on an iPad, allowing students to watch your idea take shape, every step of the way. Help them connect the dots by creating a step-by-step video that outlines your explanation in the simplest, most direct way possible.

Whether it's math, geography, or science, you'll never be at a loss on how to teach a concept when it comes to Screenchomp. Import a picture or draw your own, start the video sequencing, and get to work creating your very own video guide. This app works exactly like a screen capture program for your PC, only now you've got the functionality to instantly share, replay, or edit your movie.

Take a concept like mathematical division. With Screenchomp, you can illustrate a picture of a bunch of apples, for a theoretical example. Then, by drawing them being divided up and associating an equation with your picture, you're able to visually represent the concept of division in math. When you're done, Screenchomp allows you to start, stop, and export the video so that you can continue to use this example as needed.

Not too good at drawing? One of the added bonuses of Screenchomp is that it allows you to import pictures and doodle on them to illustrate a point instead. Great for subjects like geography, history, and science, this feature makes it even easier to make a visual point.

Because of Screenchomp, you're now able to help explain your teaching on the go, at any moment. No more searching online for an easier way to represent a subject or referring to outdated textbooks for an explanation. With Screenchomp, it's as easy as recording, sketching, and sharing.

Company: TechSmith Corporation
Size: 10.2 MB
Rating: 4.0
Appropriate for Grade Levels: 3-8

61
Show Me Interactive White Board

As technology progresses, teachers have found new and innovative ways to host a lecture and record their examples for students to copy into their notes. It started with the blackboard and then progressed to the overhead projector. Overhead projectors gave way to PC projectors, which in turn have given us smart boards. Now, there's a brand-new way to communicate your lecture notes visually: the Show Me Interactive White Board app.

This app does exactly what it's named to do and provides you with a digital whiteboard that never goes out of style in the classroom. From the moment you open this app, it begins to record your every touch, swipe, and doodle to give you a completely digital canvas for your lecture notes.

What really makes a digital whiteboard so appealing is its ability to incorporate multimedia right into your lecture. Don't fuss with multiple internet tabs on your PC projector or waste precious time waiting for a picture to load on the computer – just open everything up in Show Me Interactive White Board and let your app do the teaching.

This app features voice recording, different colored swatches for added organization and illustration, importable images, and an auto-record feature that encompasses your entire lecture. This app won't skip a beat, meaning you'll always be able to refer back to your recorded time and revisit topics that might not have been remembered otherwise.

Thanks to the reliability of this great product, you can save multiple Show Me Interactive White Board lectures within the app and export them at your convenience. And, the versatility doesn't stop there: you can also use this app to give feedback to students based on submitted work. Consider it one of the finer communication tools that a teacher can use with his or her students.

Company: Learnbat, Inc.
Size: 5.6 MB
Rating: 3.0
Appropriate for Grade Levels: 4-12

62
Sight Word Touch

Early childhood development is a huge concern in the academic community. The number of tools that are being invented to help our young students grow is expanding every day, so how do you know which tools really work to help a child develop and grow? When it comes to an app like Sight Word Touch, you can see the results of children who are developing each time they use this groundbreaking app.

Sight Word Touch does more than just pose questions and answers—it teaches on several different levels, giving your students the opportunity to hone their maturing skills on several different platforms. Learning by sight, sound, and touch means three facets of cognition are being addressed and combined to help accelerate and structure a student's basic learning skills.

The tests in Sight Word Touch can be determined manually or automatically, depending on the preferences set by the teacher. For students who need to focus on a particular subject, this app allows customized questions that target each specific area of development. For students who progress rapidly through the stages, there's a self-adjusting difficulty level that will continue to pose harder questions in an effort to stimulate more advanced thoughts.

In each stage of Sight Word Touch, a student will listen to a word, then identify that word based on a picture in the app. For example, if the word is "dig," students will hear the world verbally, then be prompted to pick from a number of other words that will offer the target word and a number of other words that look similar or feature similar letters. The goal is for developing children to become proficient at learning words based on letter and sound recognition.

There's no extent to the number words that you can program into Sight Word Touch. Pick any level of difficulty to help students develop, learn, and master phonetic sounds and visual word choices.

Company: Innovative Investments Ltd.
Size: 5.4 MB
Rating: 4.5
Appropriate for Grade Levels: K-5

63
Simple Mind+

Mind mapping is often overlooked as a creative way to spread out your thoughts in an easy to comprehend manner. Simple Mind+ takes this idea one step further and allows you to create flowing, comprehensive mind maps that can easily identify and expound upon core creative ideas. It works by helping students to literally draw their own conclusions based on an idea, forming theories along the way and broadening their knowledge of a particular topic.

Simple Mind+ works by "dragging and tagging." It starts with a central idea that's jotted down in the center of the app. From this idea, students can drag out new aspects for consideration, arranging them in a web-like structure around the main concept. For further categorization, concepts can be tagged and grouped, making them sub-topics of the main idea. The end result is a free-flowing web that all relates back to a topic that might otherwise have been convoluted in a student's mind.

Great for all ages and applicable to an infinite number of discussions, Simple Mind+ could be the tool that you've been searching for to help your classroom get jumpstarted on an idea. Use this app to identify book report ideas, address pros and cons about a particular subject, or create a longstanding discussion about a relevant issue.

Your mind maps will never become dull, thanks to the wide range of customizable options in Simple Mind+. Choose background colors, web pallets, or even shape bubbles to represent your ideas and give your mind map a theme that fits the discussion.

Teachers looking to communicate broader concepts to their classes can weave their own web of information, export it as a PDF document, or send it via email to be printed when needed. The options for sharing ideas are nearly endless when it comes to Simple Mind+.

Company: xpt Software & Consulting
Size: 5.8 MB
Rating: 4.0
Appropriate for Grade Levels: 6-12

64
Sketchbook

Sketchbook can bring out the artist in anyone and turn a mundane idea into a brand-new world of imaginative creativity. This highly detailed app was made with artists in mind, but anyone can easily pick it up and run with it in no time at all. And, with so many different features, options, and tools, you'll have no problem finding the perfect setting for any child in art class.

With school arts programs in constant question when it comes to budgets and funding, it might be time to invest in a solution that's as unique as the artists that it touches. Sketchbook offers all the functionality of a full art program, contained inside a single app. Draw, paint, charcoal, and more within this app as your students create works of art that would normally consume a plethora of art supplies.

This app focuses on the essentials of art and does away with many of the unnecessary features that other apps have, which only convolute the imagination and cause frustration when they're being used. Sketchbook does feature some of the most retailed tools on the market, however—different swatches, brushes, gradients, and an endless, infinite supply of colors.

Take your art class to the next level and watch as students who might not ever have taken an interest in art engulf themselves with imagination and expression. You'll be able to watch as students learn the basic concepts of art, like mixing colors, and expose themselves to more advanced techniques, like shading, all on their own.

Sketchbook is the modern-day teaching solution to our disappearing arts programs. Now, with this app, creativity doesn't have to suffer, and students can always express themselves with every brush, color, and different type of paper that you'd find in a traditional art room.

Company: Autodesk Inc.
Size: 32.7 MB
Rating: 4.0
Appropriate for Grade Levels: 4-12

65
Skitch

Being able to digitally annotate and mark up a document is one of the more useful tools available for a teacher. Besides taking notes on a digital document that you've read, Skitch can also be your solution to grading papers, offering feedback, or communicating directly with a student through their digitally submitted work. Thanks to this unique and highly effective app, you'll have the power to instantly and effortlessly mark up any document with pen marks, arrows, shapes, and pictures.

With more and more assignments being hosted online for students to complete, it can get tiring to constantly print and mark up these documents. Even worse, giving no feedback at all can hinder a child's ability to learn from their mistakes. By using Skitch, teachers can avoid both of these issues and present students with all of the annotations that they'd normally receive on a physical draft of their assignment. Vice versa, if you're a teacher that has shied away from using digital resources to issue and grade assignments, Skitch is an easy transition to a more advanced classroom.

Even more than just grading or marking up assignments, Skitch can be used to help your whole class learn. Thanks to this great app, you can brainstorm ideas and mark up topics in real-time, allowing students to follow along and take notes. Because it works with virtually any digital document—pictures, video, spreadsheets, documents, etc.—you'll have the power to display any resources necessary to your lesson plan.

With different colors, symbols, and the ability to customize any annotation, Skitch puts creativity in the palm of your hand. With just a few simple swipes, taps, and rotations, you can take a plain old document and transform it into something that clearly communicates your point.

Company: Evernote Corporation
Size: 10.9 MB
Rating: 4.0
Appropriate for Grade Levels: 7-12

66
Smarty

When cognitive skills are just developing and the classroom learning process begins, you're going to want the best tools possible to help students grow. Smarty is a great app for helping students discover the world around them in new and interesting ways, nurturing development, and focusing on improving basic skills. Memory and attention are two of the core focuses that Smarty works to enhance in an environment that's visually stimulating.

Attention is crucial and must always be focused when it comes to helping a child learn. Smarty does an exceptional job of keeping kids engaged through its vivid colors, cheery music, and friendly pictures. Straightforward navigation means that there won't be any confusion when it comes to operating this app—just a linear module for a child to follow and complete at their own pace.

Smarty works by playing on the idea of pictures—groups of like items, finding the odd item in a group, and identifying items based on clues. Young minds will be captivated by the attention to detail and likeable method of tapping on a picture to select it. An example of this would be to have a student pick out all of the animals in a group, leaving out those objects that are not animals. The result is a better understanding of what makes up a group and the characteristics of its objects.

In order to gauge the progress and development of a child, Smarty features a log of completed attempts after each stage of the game. This review will list the successes and failures of identifying correct objects and provide a statistical breakdown of improvement.

When it comes to encouraging development in the classroom at a young age, Smarty has everything you need. It sparks interest from students, encourages them to keep learning, and provides feedback on areas that need improvement, as well as those areas where a child excels.

Company: Smarty Pants School LLC
Size: 148 MB
Rating: 4.5
Appropriate for Grade Levels: K-4

67
Sockpuppets

Put a new-age spin on the concept of a classic puppet show with the Sockpuppets app for your iPad. This ingenious app allows your students to narrate and create their very own virtual puppet shows, complete with characters, props, and animation. Besides a great way to encourage class participation, this app focuses on social development, literacy, and conversational skills in order to help a child's communication flourish.

Different backdrops and characters make it easy to create a unique, one-of-a-kind puppet show, no matter how many times you use this app. Pick from different props and add custom animations to bring life to the puppet show and create a story that anyone can easily follow. To really encourage participation from students, have them narrate different characters for a full experience.

In students who experience social or communication difficulties, the Sockpuppets app can be a great tool in addressing and solving the problem. This informal medium of communication can be the push some students need to become vocal and share their thoughts on a larger scale.

What really sells the idea of a virtual puppet show is Sockpuppets' real-time lip-syncing features. When you tap the record button, this app will immediately recognize incoming sounds and move the puppet's lips accordingly. This can be a huge asset when dealing with children who are shy to the idea of participating in a puppet show, as it speaks to the legitimacy of the characters within the app.

Create, save, and share numerous puppet shows with Sockpuppets. This app is lightweight, fast, and flexible when it comes to classroom use. Put on a digital puppet show in your room and watch as your students jump at the chance to participate and share their thoughts and ideas.

Company: Smith Micro Software, Inc.
Size: 18.0 MB
Rating: 4.0
Appropriate for Grade Levels: 2-6

68
Socrative

Instantly engage your entire classroom and get an accurate response to any question with the Socrative app. This digital polling app allows you to ask a question to your class and elicit their feedback via a direct response. Not only that, but it also saves time on grading by automatically aggregating results for you. As a replacement for overpriced, outdated smart clicker technologies, this app can instantly expand on your classroom quizzing options.

Choose from a variety of different quizzing options, including:

Short Answer Questions: Students will be asked a question that requires them to type a custom response. Once each student has submitted their feedback, you can choose to grade the answers yourself or display them in a public forum in order to choose the best one with a vote. These questions can provoke intelligent, thoughtful insights on the question at hand.

Quick Quiz: You set the pace and have students work on a preset number of questions – just like a traditional quiz. Preprogram a batch of questions into Socrative and have the correct answers tallied up automatically for you, saving time on grading individual answers.

Create a Quiz: Import your own custom quiz questions, both multiple choice and short answer, and pick the variables that you want to define the test. Once you're done, you can set parameters and have the returned data automatically fed into results that are communicated to your students.

Space Race: Bring out the competitive nature of your classroom with this ingenious, fast-paced quiz. Questions are answered in quick succession by whoever chimes in first. Use this method to encourage quick responses and increased attention.

Multiple Choice: A traditional multiple choice quiz in a non-traditional way. Your students will be able to take a quiz that features a selection of answers, where the answers are directly reported as correct or incorrect. Socrative makes this age-old quizzing method interesting once again.

Let Socrative help you illustrate a point, ask for feedback, or gauge the overall understanding of your class – instantly and effortlessly.

Company: Socrative, Inc.
Size: 1.9 MB
Rating: 4.0
Appropriate for Grade Levels: 4-12

69
Sonic Pics Lite

This is the easiest way to make telling a story fun. Sonic Pics Lite lets you customize photos from your iPhoto library, arrange them in a slideshow and add narrative audio over them. Great for class presentations and informative reports, Sonic Pics Lite is a great way to spark the imagination of your class in a way that's both fun and engaging.

Record up to one full hour of pictures and audio commentary with this easy-to-use app. Students of all ages will effortlessly learn the ins and outs of this slideshow creator and be able to form exceptional, seamless presentations in no time at all. What's more, thanks to all of the functionality and innovation contained within this single app, you'll be able to save, export, and re-watch any presentation over and over again.

Sonic Pics Lite is wildly popular as a tool for visual reports and class lecture presentations. Teachers can arrange sample photos and record instructions on how to do just about anything. In fact, giving a digital presentation with supplemental material has never been easier—just tap the play button and watch as your lecture comes alive.

One of the best uses for Sonic Pics Lite in the classroom is video blogging. Blogs are a great way to spark enthusiasm and participation from students. What better way to make a great class blog than with unique recordings from each student in the form of a Sonic Pics light slideshow? Your class will have an excellent time creating their very own contributions with this app, with the end result being a powerful example of community learning.

Bring Sonic Pics Lite into your classroom and let the possibilities for an engaging presentation proliferate right before your eyes. With just a few photos and the will to narrate a story, you'll generate some of the best slideshows ever.

Company: Humble Daisy, Inc.
Size: 7.3 MB
Rating: 3.5
Appropriate for Grade Levels: 7-12

70
Soundrop

It's not often that you're able to teach students one concept by way of a completely different one: like teaching geometry through a lecture on gravity—it just doesn't make sense. With the Soundrop app however, this is more than ordinary: it's an excellent way to expose students to new concepts by thinking outside of the box. Support one idea with another, even though the two are seemingly unrelated.

Soundrop is a great app for students of all ages, but best suits middle and high school students who are learning about geometry and geometric shapes. The app revolves around the ability to play music by way of drawing lines—lines that eventually become complex geometrical shapes. The key is to use the concept of gravity to drop small, virtual spheres onto the lines and shapes to create sounds. Before you know it, you're playing music while learning about science and math.

The great thing about Soundrop is its ability to stimulate a student's mind in ways that normal lectures and basic examples might not. For example: what happens when you change the angle of a line: how does it affect the sound that's produced? By asking students to think critically by using an interactive example like Soundrop, you'll be pushing the bar for understanding.

Another great thing about Soundrop is its ability to be annotated for more refined examples. If you want to illustrate a particular shape or line combination and show how it reacts with other geometric shapes, simply designate it a different color. The possibilities for marking up and exemplifying different shapes are only restricted by how you choose to use them.

Bring the exceptional teaching approach of Soundrop into your classroom for an added advantage in teaching geometry and other concepts. Your students will be captivated by the melodic charm of this app, and their curiosity to understand how it works will support your lesson plan.

Company: Develoe, LLC
Size: 0.7 MB
Rating: 3.5
Appropriate for Grade Levels: 6-12

71
Story Patch

Self-expression is something that we must foster in younger students in order to help them develop socially, as well as academically. In young students especially, the imagination is an ever-active part of classroom learning—so why not foster growth by letting their imaginations run wild? Story Patch can help your students bring their fantasies to life in an interactive, easy-to-use setting designed specifically for storytelling.

This app is built on the model that children need an outlet for their everyday creative brainstorming. By giving them an entire slew of options to create their own characters, storylines, and objects, Story Patch opens the door to creative development and self-expression. In the classroom, this can be exactly what a child needs to further his or her own self-esteem and social skills.

It all starts with a blank page and your student's imagination. From there, Story Patch helps to create different characters and other essential storytelling items to get the ball rolling. Students can choose different colors, backdrops, images, and tools to best craft their own dialogue for self-expression. Story Patch also supplies a number of themes that can help a child get started with their story if they're not sure where to begin.

Because of all of these tools and the advanced platform that they're on, your students will be able to create their own story in a smarter way. This means more room for detail, which leads to better cognitive development and a higher sense of understanding when it comes to conceptualizing ideas in the future.

Save and share each story with just a few simple taps. Story Patch will export your student's masterpiece as a PDF file, which is easily printed or emailed. Encourage them to create an ongoing story or a series that focuses on a single objective to better hone their creative abilities—it's a great way to help a young student grow into a quick-learning adolescent.

Company: Haywoodsoft LLC
Size: 28.9 MB
Rating: 4.5
Appropriate for Grade Levels: K-4

72
StoryKit

Turning your young students into amateur storytellers is a great way to strengthen core-learning dependencies and promote creative expression. The StoryKit app can help spark your children's ambition to create their own fairy tales and other stories by giving them the necessary tools in an easy-to-use environment. They can illustrate, narrate, and create their own plots to successfully hone their storytelling skills and open the door for other cognitive focuses. Ask any child to tell you a story, and they can pull one from the depths of their imaginations in a heartbeat. Ask them to illustrate this story for you, and you might have less than amicable results with a bunch of crayons and some paper. Put an iPad with the StoryKit in front of them, however, and you're going to have a full-length, fully illustrated story in no time at all.

This app lets students choose between a blank slate or a commonly known fairy tale, like the Three Little Pigs. Have them craft their own story using pictures from your iPad's iPhoto app or let them retell the traditional story to their own liking—either way, their imaginations are quick at work, churning out new ideas. Through the use of various paintbrush tools, text insertions, and sound bites, you'll watch as the kids create a multimedia storytelling experience in very little time.

As your students illustrate their imaginations in the form of a shareable storybook, they'll also be developing their analytical, problem-solving, and literacy skills at the same time. In turn, by using StoryKit, you'll be helping children to acclimate themselves with real-world skills that will help them become more proficient learners in the future.

The best part about StoryKit is the fact that it gives you a custom web address for your saved stories once they've been uploaded onto the StoryKit server. Encourage your students to show their parents and share their stories with others to help build their self-esteem and nurture creative expression.

Company: University of Maryland
Size: 6.5 MB
Rating: 4.0
Appropriate for Grade Levels: 1-3

73
Storyrobe

Storyrobe by Storyrobe Inc. is the one-stop shop for students to creatively write and tell stories. The 99 cent app allows students to pick out photos and videos, either provided or uploaded, and add them to a story written by the student. A video of the story is created, with a recording of the story playing along with the images. The process is all quite simple. A student takes pictures or videos already on the iPad and puts them into a logical order for a story. Then, while recording their voices reading the story, the student flicks through the pictures. The app records both their voice and the timing of the pictures being flipped, to make a seamless video of the story. Once made, the story can be uploaded to YouTube, the Storyrobe website, or emailed to share with others, though is not necessary to save the creation.

Users of the app are for the most part very complimentary, giving it a rating of just under four stars. Many are amazed at how easy the app is to use, as it is basically a simple video editor. They also love how many different options there are to share the stories. The main complaints for the app, however, are that it has a tendency to crash while finalizing large projects and won't allow rearrangement of the pictures once they are selected. These more frustrating flaws would make this app better suited for older elementary school students and up, but with teacher supervision, younger children would have no trouble figuring it out.

But, most important, what can this app do in the classroom setting? In a one iPad room, class stories could be created—about a recent field trip, a class composed story, or recreating a story being read in class to gain a better understanding with illustrations.

Teachers can use the app to help children visualize important points in reading assignments by reconstructing the scenes. This would be helpful in all ages, as it can be adjusted by the teacher creating the story insofar as the difficulty in words used and speed of the reading.

In classrooms with multiple iPads available, groups can be assigned to do similar things—create original tales using the imagination of the team or remake passages from class books. This would give teachers and students more freedom in what they made, as teachers could walk around and help more children to be sure they understand all parts of the assignment, and it gives the students a more hands-on learning experience. The creations could then be uploaded to the Storyrobe website or brought to the front of the room on the iPad to share with the rest of the class. This method would work better for older elementary students and up, as younger children may not know how to work the iPad effectively, and the amount of teacher supervision necessary would perhaps hinder the learning experience for the children, instead of enhancing it.

Finally, in classrooms where iPads are available for all the students, children could do the same activities but on an individual level. The amount of independence this would give students would mean this teaching method would be better suited for mature elementary school kids or even only middle school students and up. The videos, again, could be shared online or by bringing the iPad to the front of the room.

Company: Storyrobe Inc.
Size: 6.3 MB
Rating: 3.7 Stars
Grade Level: All

74
StoryTime

Books are an invaluable tool to encourage literacy competency and analytical skills among developing children. More often than not, books are used to help teach kids in the classroom in the form of book reports, class read-alongs, and independent study. But your classroom might not have all of the books you'd like it to have. The solution? The StoryTime book app gives you an infinite number of great books to share with your class in order to encourage reading.

Choose from favorite publishers like McGraw Hill, Kane Miller, and other educationally-focused publishers to ensure that your students always have a good book to put their nose in… or rather their finger on when it comes to iPad reading. You'll be able to download these books straight to the app, creating your own virtual library of great titles that might not be readily available in your nearest library. Cheaper than buying and more convenient than renting, StoryTime is the way to go if you're looking for a good read.

Where StoryTime really shines is in its ability to support multimedia enhancement. This means that, in addition to the book, you'll also have access to special features for each title, such as read along audio cues, simple animations, and more. Together, these extra features can make a story come to life, right before your class' eyes.

In the digital age of technology that we're living in, it can be easy to forget the joy of books. Don't let technology overpower the will to use a good book during class, but at the same time, don't live in the Stone Age when it comes to storytelling. Meet somewhere in the middle and use StoryTime to engage your kids with a great read.

Company: Teknowledge Software
Size: 23.2 MB
Rating: 3.5
Appropriate for Grade Levels: 2-6

75
StudyBlue

Whether you teach kindergarten or college, flashcards are one of the best tools in your arsenal for helping students study and learn different topics. Sometimes, however, flashcards can get to be a big mess and be hard to carry from place to place all at one time. StudyBlue has the solution to this problem and gives you a plentiful list of features that can turn your student's flashcards into easy-to-carry, powerful learning tools.

This flashcard app has the ability to support hundreds of decks of flashcards, with thousands of cards in each deck, giving unlimited possibilities when it comes to programming in different facts and vocabulary words. It works just like a normal flashcard would: displaying a question on one side and the answer on the other. To see the answer, just tap the flashcard and watch it flip on command.

StudyBlue is all about gauging your progress and how far you've come since creating a specific deck of cards. The app will tell you how many cads are in a deck, when the deck was created, an analysis of how many you got right or wrong and the percent that you've progressed since last quizzing yourself. As if that wasn't useful enough, StudyBlue also tracks your record with each individual card, giving a history of right and wrong guesses and the frequency of correct guesses.

No traditional flashcard can give your students the insight and information that this app does. Plus, because all of the information is contained in a handy mobile app, you can encourage students to study anywhere. Whether it's on the bus, in study hall, or waiting in line at the store, StudyBlue can easily become an instant study buddy.

Encourage your students to download this free study supplement: it's worth their while and incredibly easy to use. StudyBlue contains everything a student needs to brush up on course topics… it's like a virtual backpack.

Company: StudyBlue, Inc.
Size: 15.5 MB
Rating: 4.5
Appropriate for Grade Levels: K-12

76
TeacherPal

Who needs a teaching assistant when you've got TeacherPal? When it comes to recording grades, marking attendance, and noting behavior, this app does in minutes what it might take you an hour or more to do. It's at the forefront of teacher assistance technology and can be your saving grace when it comes to keeping track of your students.

TeacherPal has a variety of great tools to keep you up to speed with your class and individual students, including:

Attendance Records: Mark students as present, sick, absent, or tardy with a single tap of your finger. Designate your own tags to categorize different statuses for each of your students, then check back in your records to see their history over weeks and months. You'll be able to instantly tell where a student was just by looking them up in TeacherPal's database.

Face Mapping: Is it hard for you to memorize names right away? Fine-tune your name memorization skills by taking small snapshots of students and assigning them to names within TeacherPal. Soon, you'll have names associated with faces and won't have to struggle to recall a student's name. What's more, you can even assign them to a specific desk chart, allowing you to further inform yourself about who's who.

Grade Records: Recording a grade is easier than ever when it comes to TeacherPal. This app allows you to enter grades for individual students and keep a running log of their work. Just export the data when you're ready to use it elsewhere; otherwise, keep it securely hidden within the app.

Designate Subjects: Do you have different classes? Teach different subjects? TeacherPal supports a variety of different designations that allow you to make different profiles for your various classes. You'll be able to keep everything straight by easily flipping back and forth between classes.

Do away with the grade book, attendance sheets, and seating charts. Use TeacherPal instead—it has everything you rely on to keep your class running smoothly, and best of all, it's completely secure.

Company: ITWorx
Size: 12.7 MB
Rating: 4.0
Appropriate for Grade Levels: 6-12

77
TED

If you're familiar with TED Talks, you'll know that they cover some of the most interesting topics known to man, as seen by some of the most remarkable people in the world. Now, you can bring these innovative, groundbreaking segments into your classroom in a way that's easy for you to share with your students. The TED app contains all of the most talked about, riveting speeches that have made TED Talks famous.

Whether it's a social issue, scientific topic, or something more, the TED app is sure to have a lecture that will stimulate the minds of your class and provoke plenty of questions or discussion. If you're looking for a specific subject, you can even search the app for the perfect video.

Thanks to the great functionality of this app, you can create custom playlists and view different categories of video just by tapping and swiping. If you're looking to bridge the gap between lecture topics or help students freely associate two different ideas, consider bridging the gap with a video from the TED app.

Not only are these riveting talks engaging and easy to understand, but they're given by experts that truly understand the topic at hand—so you're hearing great information straight from those who know it firsthand. There's no better source for educational videos and no better way to access them than this valuable app.

Begin each class with an insightful TED Talk to stimulate discussion or save them for lecture days; the choice is yours. No matter how you use the TED app, just know that you're exposing your students to some of the best knowledge on groundbreaking ideas and traditional issues.

The TED app is updated weekly to include brand-new talks and extended content, so you'll never have to worry about running out of lecture materials. Keep this exceptional teaching tool in mind the next time you're searching for supplemental content in your discussions.

Company: TED Conferences
Size: 12.0 MB
Rating: 4.5
Appropriate for Grade Levels: 8-12

78
ThreeRing

The ability to keep track of a student's work is important to consider as a teacher. Oftentimes, you'll need to give feedback on a grade, make comments on an assignment, or make copies of work to share. Don't let stacks of paper assignments and a cluster of digital files drag you down—instead, keep perfect tabs on all of your assignments with the ThreeRing app.

By using your iPhone or iPad camera, you'll be able to take perfect pictures of a student's submitted work in order to archive and store it safely for later use. What's more, ThreeRing gives you the option to organize these archives in several different formats, including by student, class, and tag.

If you're managing multiple classes or several subjects, it can be difficult to keep copies of everyone's work. Luckily, ThreeRing not only gives you a way to store assignments, but organize them, as well. No matter how complex your system is, this app will be able to provide precise organizational categories to keep your method working fluidly.

Pictures, video, digital files, and audio notes can all be added to ThreeRing to help supplement each student's digital portfolio. Plus, you can make checklists and groups to mark off completed work, outstanding assignments, or incompletions. Keep track of a child's consistency online and keep yourself in the loop about who's on track and who could use some encouragement.

Never before has there been a way to command so much information in one place. This app gives you everything you need to be instantly informed about a student and their history of work in your class. Whether it's retrieving completed assignments for review, addressing a concern about a missing piece, or watching the progression of a student, ThreeRing has it all.

Company: Three Ring
Size: 2.5 MB
Rating: 4.5
Appropriate for Grade Levels: 4-12

79
Times Tables

Times tables have always been a great way to help teach students multiplication easily and rhythmically. But where flashcards and charts once paved the way for learning multiplication, they're being replaced with more up-to-date methods—like the Times Tables app for iPhone or iPad. It serves the same function as traditional materials, but gives you the ability to encourage learning in a customizable, interactive environment.

Times Tables gives students a set number of questions with the ability to add a time limit. In each instance, they'll be given a multiplication problem and a set of possible answers. Correct answers will be marked with a gold star, while incorrect ones will be given a red circle. At the end of each sequence, your student will be given an evaluation of all of their answers, as well as a summary of their progress.

What makes this app great is its ability to identify which sets of numbers your student is having an issue with. For example, if factors of seven seem to be harder for a child, you'll be able to see these problems in a summary report. What's more, once you've identified problem numbers, you can create custom question sets to help a student practice.

For students who pick up multiplication quickly, you can challenge them further by reversing problems. For example, if they know automatically that "6 x 4 = 24," you can switch up the problem to read "4 x 6 = ?" to foster the growth of problem solving and analytical skills. The options that Times Tables gives you are excellent for this key area of mathematical learning.

To keep it interesting, this app adds features like high scores and best times. Have your students race to beat their best time while still remaining accurate, or add more problems to the set to build up a top score that can't be beat. Students will love learning their multiplication tables with the Times Tables app.

Company: Rob Clarke
Size: 4.2 MB
Rating: 3.5
Appropriate for Grade Levels: 3-6

80
Today in History

When it comes to history, dates can be the hardest things for a student to remember. Help engrain the importance of timelines and specific dates with help from the Today in History app for iPhone. Besides giving you some of the most important, newsworthy pieces of information in history, this app will associate them with specific dates and times to help you give your students a better understanding of historical importance.

With over 100,000 historical moments preprogrammed into this app, you'll have no shortage of interesting facts to share with your class about how the world has shaped itself over time. Use these centralized thoughts to spark discussion, pose historical questions, and bolster your class' knowledge of history.

Want to know what was happening around the world on any given day? Today in History will give you a complete historical profile when it comes to what the world was doing and where it was being done. By illustrating different events in a fantastic historical context, this app will provide the basis for learning historically-relevant information and applying it to modern-day discussions.

Best of all, this app functions as a teaching tool for dates and linear timelines. Instead of asking students to simply memorize different dates and times, you can give them content and comparisons to help with date memorization. The cohesion of events and times does wonders for teaching history.

Today in History shines where other history apps don't by offering you more than just information. This app also allows you to program in your own events and data to give more perspective on different historical events. For example, if you're teaching the French revolution, why not program in important dates for your students to learn? They'll be able to see what happened on key dates, in sequence and in detail.

Choose Today in History for teaching history in a newer, smarter way—one day at a time.

Company: Doapp, Inc.
Size: 15.8 MB
Rating: 4.0
Appropriate for Grade Levels: 6-12

81
Today in History Lite

Every classroom has a history buff. Whether it's you or a student, they're bound to exist. They tend to know everything about most topics you discuss, sometimes more than their teacher. Their knowledge can overpower some of the other students. By downloading the Today in History Lite app, everyone can be included in the new information learned. Who knows, maybe even the class' history buff will learn something.

Each time you open the Today in History Lite app, the main page includes all the noteworthy events of that day by years. These events can go back hundreds of years and are very easy to scroll through to get a brief overview. By clicking on any event, you can get a more in-depth description. The app also provides multiple, sometimes more than three, external links that send you to other sites for even more explanation. Depending on the importance or how well known the event is, the amount of links can vary. To make things even more fun, you can also create your own private events to share with friends and family. With over 100 thousand different events, everybody can learn something new.

All classrooms that deal with history to some extent can have fun with the Today in History Lite app. If there is only one iPad in the classroom, you can read the list of events for the day to the entire class. Students can then pick one or more of these events on which to write or comment. By doing this, they can continue to learn and reflect on other things besides what they are learning about in class. If there are multiple iPads, students can read up on the event on their own. For classes where everyone has their own iPad, they can even go home and work on the write-up as an actual assignment. They can also look up events that happen over the weekend.

Today in History Lite doesn't have to be used only for the specific events of the day. You can also search for various events by name in the app. Then you can view the same description and links that you would see from the actual list by day. Students can use this feature as another way to get research for projects and assignments. Your classroom can also create events into the apps. These events can be the birthdates of other classmates and teachers so everyone knows when they are.

For every trivia, knowledge, and history lover, Today in History Lite is a must-have app. Students of all ages will be able to learn something about our world's past. The lite version is free, and you can upgrade to get rid of the apps within. By using this app, you can give even the classroom history buff a run for their money.

Company: Manuel Zamora
Size: 10.8 MB
Rating: 4.5 Stars
Grade Level: All

82
Toontastic

Children are natural storytellers—it's part of their creative expression and can help them develop the skills they need to excel in other areas of their education. Nourish your students' imagination and help them discover their true storytelling potential with the Toontastic app.

Apart from being a premier way for your students to create, illustrate, and animate their own stories, this app is also a key tool in helping develop fundamental skills associated with storytelling. Vocabulary, linear thought, and other multiple-literacy skills are all enriched when it comes to storytelling with Toontastic. From the very moment a student creates a character, all the way to the summation of their tale, you'll be able to watch as these core areas of focus are addressed.

Toontasic offers a valuable tool that other storytelling apps don't: the story arc. This visual representation of how a story is formed will help your students recognize the different parts of a story and how they function in relation to one another. Have your kids identify the introduction, rising action, climax, falling action, and the resolution of their story with help from this exceptional storytelling tool.

Animate characters by just moving your fingers or draw your very own items easily with the built-in editor to make the most out of your story. Pick a different theme, depending on the settings, or import your own pictures for a custom fairy tale. When you're done, title your masterpiece and upload it to the Internet to share with other storytellers all around the world.

With so many ways to enrich a child's imagination, there's no reason not to use a great app like Toontastic for classroom learning. You'll create an exciting environment for children to learn basic literary skills, while providing them with the ability to watch their own thoughts take shape in a way that's never been done before.

Company: Launchpad Toys
Size: 130 MB
Rating: 4.5
Appropriate for Grade Levels: K-4

83
Totes m'Notes

The best way to encourage good note-taking is to make the process interesting and fun. The Totes m'Notes app will instantly engage your students and task them with taking good notes in a customizable, user-friendly environment. With so many different possibilities, this app can create a one-of-a-kind notebook for any student.

The way Totes m'Notes works is simple—just create a customized notebook from a variety of different themes or upload a picture from your iPhoto. From there, you'll have the ability to designate subjects, mark up content, and take good, clean notes for any class. Different notebooks are stored on a virtual bookshelf, allowing you to easily access previous notes to study or share.

Students can type or doodle their notes, allowing them to create a familiar, friendly journal of their learning. When it comes to subjects that require diagrams or drawn examples, Totes m'Notes makes it easy to sketch a picture, right in the notes. You can even annotate different pages with stickers or color codes for instant review possibilities.

Label and date notes in Totes m'Notes and enable the app to search through your notes for instant results. No more flipping through pages in a three-subject notebook or scavenging through your backpack to find a single missing page. This app saves notes on the go, so they're always available.

If you want to encourage good note-taking in your classroom, consider the benefits of Totes m'Notes. It's digital, which can be an easier medium for some kids to navigate, accessible and customizable to a number of degrees. It encourages kids to use their own creativity and organizational skills to take and keep good notes. Plus, with everything available in a single place, students are less inclined to misplace or lose their notes.

Company: The Incredible Minotaurs LLC
Size: 126 MB
Rating: 3.5
Appropriate for Grade Levels: 4-12

84
Twitter

Twitter is a social networking site that has exploded in popularity in recent years. Naturally, there's an app to go with it. Twitter allows you to browse interests, find/follow friends like your average social network site, "tweet" your own information, and favorite and follow interests. It also is a great way to see topics, such as breaking news or sports. As a user, you can also share photos and videos with your followers.

Twitter is free and reviews at three stars out of five. The app was rated higher, but recent versions have slowed it down, and thus the rating went down, as well.

Entering the app, there are groups of topics offered along the side such as family, news, television, etc. By clicking on the category, the app reveals recent tweets made by varying officials, celebrities, or just the average Joe voicing information or opinions on the subject. By clicking on "Twitter" at the top of the home page, the user is directed to the top tweet and popular topics of the day. The user, whether teacher or student, can also decide to make an account. This gives them the option to tweet their own information, as well as upload photos or videos. They can also follow certain topics or people. They are then alerted when that person tweets something.

This app, while seemingly the average social site, can be applied to the classroom. If the teacher has access to a single iPad, it can be used to talk about and share news and events that happened, whether done daily or weekly. Another option is to pick a topic and have students debate and form an opinion on the subject. Teachers can also have an account in which they can post videos of them teaching a lesson or doing example problems, so students can view them at home if they were gone or just need more reinforcement. If a couple of iPads are available, students can form groups to find information on an assigned topic and report it to the class or look at current events. If students all have access to an iPad, they can all make accounts and follow the teacher. This would allow a student to ask a question out of school or for video projects to be posted for grading. Students can also find an interesting trend and write a quick paragraph on the subject, increasing their writing skills, as well as their awareness of what's going on in the world around them.

Twitter gives students and teachers another way to communicate quickly and conveniently outside of school. It also opens students' eyes to the news in quick, 140 character messages. This summary is quicker than the news, thus is more appealing to the average student.

Company: Twitter, Inc.
Size: 12 MB
Rating: 3
Age: 5th grade and up

85
Viddy

Visual teaching is one of the most effective ways to stimulate a child's mind. Give them information on a topic and provide visual supplements to solidify the concept. The downside to visual teaching is that if you're not careful, you could lose students in the process if they become bored or preoccupied with other features of a video. That's where Viddy comes in—this app is short and to the point, giving your kids information through video, without all of the extra distractions.

Much like Twitter's limit on characters, Viddy has a limit on a video's time length. Because of this time restriction, videos make a bigger impression on students because they're short, to the point, and explicitly informational. To further this idea, videos can be tagged and uploaded to the Internet so that you can find exactly what you're looking for.

But Viddy isn't just about watching; it's about filming, as well. Because videos are limited to 15 seconds, you can easily use this app right in class to involve it in the teaching process. Say, for instance, that you're giving a lecture on gravity and part of your lecture involves dropping an egg from a height that will surely break it. If you've got the Viddy app handy, you can film this experiment for the few seconds that it takes to perform it and have that video on hand to replay—which is especially great for instances that require an explanation or elaboration.

Want to discover other short video clips that can help bring light to a subject that you're teaching? Search Viddy's huge database of user-uploaded videos to view any number of other videos that fit your needs. Because every video is short and highly specific to a topic, you'll be able to show multiple examples to better communicate the point.

Company: Viddy, Inc.
Size: 19.0 MB
Rating: 4.0
Appropriate for Grade Levels: 4-12

86
Video Science

What's better than step-by-step instructions for cool classroom science experiments in the palm of your hand? How about a growing library of over 80 instructional videos that show you how to perform these experiments in real time? The Video Science app has exactly that and can be a great complement to your science classroom. With plenty of experiments on a vast gamut of topics, Video Science opens the door to a whole new batch of resources to help teach your students about science.

Narrated precisely and thoroughly by Dan Menelly, a Science Teacher at the UN International School and a 2010 Einstein Fellow with the National Science Foundation in the Office of Cyberinfrastructure, you're guaranteed to have a great time doing these experiments. Each featured video gives you background on the experiment that's being performed, materials required, and the amount of time needed to complete the procedure.

If you're looking for a specific video to show your class, it's easy to find in the Video Science app library. You can search by episode, category, or scroll through the featured videos to find the one you're looking for. Once you've found it, add it to your favorites for later so you can easily bring it up and re-watch it.

With the Video Science app, you're given the peace of mind that every experiment you watch is one hundred percent safe to perform in your class. Because this app is geared toward teachers, it follows only the safest guidelines and will preemptively warn you about any factors in an experiment that might be dangerous. You'll never have to worry about an experiment going wrong if you follow the directions and take heed to the visual and audial commands given by the host.

Bring new experiments into your classroom and captivate your students with hands-on, physical learning from Video Science.

Company: Science House Foundation
Size: 17.9 MB
Rating: 4.0
Appropriate for Grade Levels: 6-12

87
Voice Memos

Verbal dictation is important to master as a teacher because it's how you'll spend most of your days communicating with students. Getting your point across the first time is crucial, so make sure you've laid out precisely what you're trying to say. The Voice Memos app can help you make sure what you're trying to communicate is exactly what you're saying.

This handy app works great in a number of tasks that involve speaking and can offer you the chance to record, listen, and edit your own words:

Verbal Note-taking: Want to take notes on something for your personal review later? If you don't have time to stop and write, consider recording your thoughts. Voice Memos runs in the background on your iPad or iPhone, allowing you to do other things while still recording your voice. It can be great for noting ideas that you have while surfing the web, watching a video, or looking through your grades.

Give Instruction: Do you have a complex set of instructions that need to be communicated more than just once? Record them with Voice Memos and email them to your students. They'll be able to listen as many times as they need to in order to understand the task at hand. This also works for things like group projects and research assignments.

Record a Lecture: If you're going to be out of class for a while, it can be helpful to prepare your lectures ahead of time. With Voice Memos, this is as easy as talking to your iPad while it records a full lecture for you. Better yet, if you've got a student who is going to be out of class for an extended period of time, record the lecture for them so that they don't miss out on a learning opportunity.

If it involves speaking or communication, Voice Memos is the end all, be all of apps. This invaluable tool for recording and editing your thoughts will prove itself useful time and time again.

Company: KendiTech Inc.
Size: 6.2 MB
Rating: 4.0
Appropriate for Grade Levels: 7-12

88
VoiceThread

Do you have something important to talk about? Of course, you do. Share it with everyone who's willing to listen with the help of the VoiceThread app. This great application allows you to talk about your topic while offing visual supplements to a listener for the best learning experience possible.

VoiceThread works like this: you pick an image, a video clip, or a combination of both and load it into the app. From there, you record your thoughts on the topic at hand, changing the image or video clip as you go to better illustrate your point. When you're all done, save your thread and export it—or upload it to the vast VoiceThread server to share it with others who might want to listen.

In the classroom, this app is more valuable than ever. Not only does it give you the chance to teach a lesson through a multimedia platform, it also gives you access to a humongous library of other threads just like yours—some with different twists on the same topic for added exposure.

During your video, you can even mark up the screen to further illustrate a point or call attention to a specific detail. Keep your students engaged with a variety of different pictures or video clips that flow seamlessly with your lecture and draw on VoiceThread's creative tools to keep your display unique.

If you register for a VoiceThread account, the app will automatically save and store your threads in a way that's easy to categorize and search. Record an entire series on a single subject or interject shorter threads into your regular discussion to emphasize special points. You'll keep coming back to VoiceThread's great interface to record your lectures: it's an easy-to-use, visually effective tool that anyone can take advantage of.

Company: VoiceThread
Size: 1.8 MB
Rating: 3.5
Appropriate for Grade Levels: 4-12

89
Whiteboard

Whiteboard is the final frontier of whiteboard apps. The numerous features, displays, design tools, and abilities that make themselves present in this tool offer you a world of features that not even a physical whiteboard can match. No matter what subject you teach or who you're going to be collaborating with, this app is sure to give you exactly what you need to communicate clearly and thoroughly.

Here are just a few of the different features that make Whiteboard a sensational app for classrooms and teachers:

Jotting Ideas: Whether you prefer to draw them with traditional dry erase markers or want to use more interactive means to plot your point, Whiteboard supports your creative expressions in a variety of different ways. In no time at all, you'll be able to put your thoughts on your virtual whiteboard and watch them take shape for others to collaborate with or learn from.

Sharing: Want to involve a group of people or maybe even your whole class in your discussion? Whiteboard offers screen sharing and live board sharing over a Wi-Fi network, making it easy to involve everyone in the discussion. Participants can mark up the shared board or just look on to see your administrative changes, making for an all-inclusive conversation that benefits everyone involved.

Easy File Transfer: Once you've finished with a discussion on a physical whiteboard, it gets wiped down and restored to a blank slate. With the Whiteboard app, however, you can save your doodles, designs, and discussions for a later date by sending them to your PC or uploading them to DropBox. Print them off for even easier sharing and make sure everyone is in the loop.

Using Whiteboard in your classroom is a smart step in an interactive direction. By involving students in the virtual discussion and encouraging them to participate, you'll have more students focusing on learning and less on other things.

Company: Splashtop Inc.
Size: 18.5 MB
Rating: 4.5
Appropriate for Grade Levels: 4-12

90
WhiteBoard Lite Collaborative

Whiteboards have become a staple for learning in classrooms around the globe: chances are you've even used one yourself, complete with an assortment of different colored markers. Now, you can have this same teaching experience in a digital environment, thanks to the Whiteboard Lite Collaborative app. Use it just like a real whiteboard for any teaching endeavor you might have, and wipe it magically clean when it's time to start over.

Choose from any color under the sun to doodle with, and keep a number of colors handy in your pallet for a seamless drawing experience. The Whiteboard Lite Collaborative app gives you all of the tools you need to mark up your virtual whiteboard, right at your fingertips. Plus, you'll never have to worry about a marker going bad… because your finger is the marker.

Whiteboard Lite Collaborative has more possibilities than first meets the eye, however. Sure, you can use it as a way to mark up a math problem or doodle a diagram for a scientific concept, but this app is also capable of peer-to-peer communication, as well. Connect with individual students in your room and have them participate along with you to make sure that they understand concepts and can execute ideas properly.

With such an easy-to-use, two-way form of communication, this app makes its value known instantly. As an open channel for questions, answers, and feedback, there's no telling what you can accomplish with your students. Make your classroom a virtual discussion board with the Whiteboard Lite Collaborative app today.

When you're done with a lecture, picture, or collaborate board, save it and send it to your computer—it's just that easy. Where a physical whiteboard can be erased, the virtual Whiteboard Lite Collaborative app can always be saved for another day.

Company: GreenGar Studios
Size: 8.1 MB
Rating: 4.0
Appropriate for Grade Levels: 4-12

91
YouTube

In this day and age, everyone has heard of YouTube—it's the world's second largest search engine, second only to Google, and has over 800 billion users who visit the site each month. What's really phenomenal about YouTube, however, is the millions of hours of video that are uploaded to it each day—video that can teach your class anything about everything.

The YouTube app is your direct link to nearly every video ever published on the Internet. Just by searching different keywords, terms, authors, or subjects, you're able to scroll through an infinite supply of visual supplements to help you teach a class about anything. With so many different options out there, you're bound to find the visual companion you need to better illustrate your concepts.

The YouTube app isn't just about searching for videos, though; it's also about uploading and sharing your own. If you're a teacher that benefits from filming lectures or inviting group participation in video formats, you'll love the uploading features that this app boasts. All you need is a YouTube user name and an Internet connection to start uploading videos to your very own channel.

Compile videos from your favorite subjects, unique authors, or just videos that are entertaining and save them to your favorites section for quick access later. You can send direct links to your students and have them watch from home, on the go, or anywhere else that they can access the Internet.

YouTube's format is simple enough to use, even if you've never been on the site before, and can quickly be mastered by you and your students. Think of it like your very own personal library of information—a source that never runs out of new content and can always be searched to find exactly what you're looking for.

Company: Lifecom
Size: 11.3 MB
Rating: 3.5
Appropriate for Grade Levels: 4-12

92
Zapd

Creating a website is easier than ever with the Zapd app. No need for coding, programming, or any other technical related tooling: just a few clicks, some photos, and good text will give you a great website in minutes. Share it online or from one device to another seamlessly. With the power to create a website made easy, you'll have no problem at all putting up a hub for students to visit.

Choose from over 20 different themes to mock up your website and customize it with any text, links, or images you want. Once you've got your Zapd website all set up, uploading is as simple as clicking a button and receiving your own unique URL.

Use your brand-new website as a class tool: for hosting assignments, segmenting your class into groups, or offering supplemental course information that isn't readily available in class. Because it's so easy to use and you can host an infinite number of Zapd sites, you'll always be able to properly communicate via this great technological tool.

When it comes to student participation, Zapd is also a great engagement tool. You can use it to host third party surveys or quizzes to encourage class participation. Take it even further by assigning a website design project to students and let them use Zapd to put up their own sites. It's easy enough for anyone to use, yet still gives you the high quality look and feel of a hardcoded website.

Zapd is a fantastic app for a quick and easy supplement to your course material. If you've always wished for an external website to post messages, reminders, assignments, and feedback, Zapd can help you get started in a jiffy. Let your creativity run free and your students reap the benefits.

Company: PressPlane Inc.
Size: 13.9 MB
Rating: 4.0
Appropriate for Grade Levels: 7-12